realization that there are two voices in life, the voice of Shadow and the voice of Spirit. It was through his 'wisdom to know the difference' between the two that led him to the 12-step path of recovery. Ultimately, this would lead him to author the book *GOD REALIZATION*. This book not only compliments the 12-step program, it evolves it by distilling the essence of religion and recovery to one principle: that by transcending the ego, Spirit is realized. May this book be a guiding light for students and teachers alike on the path toward God Realization and Self Actualization."

—Rev. Kirsten Wolfe, Interfaith Minister, LMHC

GOD
REALIZATION

THE GOD TRILOGY

BOOK 1 – GOD IS
BOOK 2 – GOD REALIZATION
coming soon:
BOOK 3 – GOD HEALS

THE COMPANION TO
THE GOD TRILOGY

GOD SPEAKS

GOD REALIZATION

Learn To Listen To The Voice Of Love

The Gospel
of
Rev. Phil

A Spiritual Guidebook

The God Trilogy — Book 2

Rev. Philip Strom

Church of the One God

Published 2021 by Reverend Philip Strom
Church of the One God
1503 Llano Street, Suite A-4
Santa Fe, NM 87505
www.churchoftheonegod.org

First edition 2021 by Church of the One God
Printed in the United States of America

Library of Congress Control Number: 2021913003

ISBN-13:   978-0-9989524-4-4 (Regular Print/Paperback)
                978-0-9989524-5-1 (Large Print/Paperback)
                978-0-9989524-6-8 (eBook/Kindle)
                978-0-9989524-7-5 (eBook/Epub)

Editors: Annie Woods and Linda J. Miller
Cover and Layout Design: Dree Morin, Dreemer Designs
www.dreemerdesigns.com
Contributing Artist/Artwork: Linda J. Miller/Third Eye Chakra

Contents

PRELUDE

"Man's ultimate aim is the realization of God and all his activities: social, political, religious, have to be guided by the ultimate aim of the vision of God. The immediate service of all human beings becomes a necessary part of the endeavor, simply because the only way to find God is to see Him in his creation and be one with it. This can only be done by service of [to?] all. I am a part and parcel of the whole and I cannot find Him apart from the rest of humanity. My countrymen are my nearest neighbors. They have become so helpless, so resource less, so inert that I must concentrate myself on serving them. If I could persuade myself that I could find Him in a Himalayan cave I would proceed there immediately. But I know that I cannot find Him apart from humanity."

Mahatma Gandhi *Harijan*, 29-8-'36

THE STORY OF REV. PHIL AND CHURCH OF THE ONE GOD

I am Reverend Philip Strom, the Spiritual Director for Church of the One God and am both an Ordained Transdenominational, Interfaith, Non-Congregational Minister and a State of New Mexico Licensed Alcohol Drug Abuse Counselor.

These two credentials were both made possible because of my engagement in a Twelve Step recovery program that helped me address and place in remission my drug addiction problems. With God's blessing and my continued involvement in my own recovery, I have not found the need to take any mood and/or mind-altering substances since August 17, 1987. During my time in recovery I have seen how the spiritual principles that the Twelve Steps are based upon and have encouraged change, not only my life but the lives of countless other individuals who actively participate in the program.

My ordination means that I honor all paths that lead to the unknowable Supreme Consciousness. It is my belief that all things in and of this universe are creations of and are at one with the Creator. Like human children being placed in a school by their parents, as children of God, our souls choose to be placed on this dimensional school plane called Earth, always with the approval of Divine Love and Wisdom. We are here to learn certain lessons that once learned will allow us to create a Heaven on Earth and function as the equal of our Creator. My mission is to help facilitate this by teaching spirituality to anyone who requests it.

In 1997 I was a working as a counselor at a State of New Mexico-funded adolescent treatment center in Santa Fe, named La Nueva Vida (LNV). LNV was an eight – to ten-month residential program for both male and female adolescents diagnosed as Level II (substance abusers). Managed Care came to New Mexico and LNV was reassigned as a Level III (mental health problems) two - to three-week program, with the possibility of a renewal period of an additional two to three weeks.

This change made two things extremely clear to me. The first was that I was no longer going to be a counselor. My job would become a combination babysitter, chauffeur and police officer. The second was that the adolescents and their families, particularly from the middle class or lower class, were not going to be serviced as they had been, which would create a great deal of suffering. I stayed at LNV long enough to graduate my clients and then I resigned.

During the end times I had numerous conversations, with my wife Lin and trusted friends, regarding what my focus for the future should be. It was suggested that I open a treatment center of my own. I rejected that idea for two reasons. The first reason was that the treatment center would be subjected to State of New Mexico oversight, by the same agencies that created the dysfunction I was attempting to get away from. The second reason was that I would wind up in a management role which would take me away from what I thought was my gift and purpose: counseling.

The outcome of these conversations was that I decided to become an ordained minister, open a counseling office and provide spiritual counseling on a donation basis. The concept of becoming an ordained minister was extremely appealing on two fronts. The first front being my belief that Twelve Step spirituality was producing better outcomes than the traditional therapeutic modalities the State was mandating to be used; the second front was that as a Minister I was, for the most part, protected from government interference in my practice by the First Amendment which separates church and state.

I embarked on the twin missions of becoming an Ordained Minister and founding an umbrella organization for my ministry. I received my ordination on September 15, 1997 from the New Mexico Theological Seminary. Church of the One God met the requirements for obtaining tax-exempt 501(c)(3) status as a religious charitable organization from the Internal Revenue Service and temporary exemption was granted on August 27, 1998 and made permanent on January 29, 2003.

I was initially going to name the organization Church of the Twelfth Step because of the transformative power I experienced from working the Twelve Steps. I backed off from that name because I believed it would violate the Traditions that guide Twelve Step fellowships and would create confusion as to who I was and what I did. I was then inspired to name the organization the name it carries to this day, Church of the One God. This name reflects the lessons I absorbed in my studies. I came to believe that all religions were designed to take the follower to the same destination. The religions differed in ritual and dogma but the further one advanced in the religion the more the religion was indistinguishable from any other. For a more in-depth explanation of this concept check out Aldous Huxley's *The Perennial Philosophy*.

With the help of my beautiful and talented wife, Lin, the first Church of the One God logo, seen below was created.

In 1999, again with Lin's help, the second rendition of the Church of the One God logo, seen below, was created. Not only were the symbols changed but they were sequenced to reflect my understanding of the ages, from oldest to youngest, left to right, of the religions they represented.

In the latter part of 2003, with Lin's assistance, the third and current version of the Church of the One God logo, seen below, was created. The logo was, in early 2015, graphically cleaned up and enhanced by my website designer and graphic designer, Dree Morin, http://www.dreemerdesigns.com

The individual symbols and their meaning are shown on the following pages.

Om is the symbol for the Hindu religion. Though it is used in other religions such as Buddhism, Jainism, and Sikhism, its first appearance is in the Vedanta texts titled the Vedas. It has many interpretations. The one I favor is that it represents the sound of Brahman (God) coming into existence.

The above is the Chinese symbol for the Tao, representing the religion of Taoism. The word Tao translates to "The Way" or to quote Wikipedia "it denotes the principle that is both the source, pattern, and substance of everything that exists."

The Star of David is a symbol of Judaism, representing the Jewish religion. It is believed that this symbol was on a magic shield owned by King David and that it protected him from his enemies. This symbol also appears on the flag of Israel.

The religion of Buddhism utilizes numerous configurations of The Buddha. The one above is known as Calling the Earth to Witness, and it represents the moment Buddha obtained enlightenment.

The cross, the most familiar symbol of the Christian religion, comes in a variety of configurations and styles. The one above is known as the Latin Cross. Though it might be the most widely recognized religious symbol, the origins of the Cross predate the Christian adaptation.

The Islamic religion is represented by the above written Arabic calligraphy symbol which represents the name Allah. In the Abrahamic religions Allah is the word for God. The most common meaning in the English language generally refers to the God of the Islamic religion. The name Allah is believed to be derived from the word al-ilāh, which means "the god", and is related to the names El and Elah, the Hebrew and Aramaic words for God.

AUTHOR'S NOTE

Blessings & Greetings,

How do we relate to God? Do we believe we have direct access to The Creator anytime, anywhere? Do we believe that The Divine Presence will always respond to our requests for guidance? Do we listen to the first responder, that small, still voice of Spirit? Or do we listen to the guidance provided by the ego/self-will/shadow? Do we even know that we have two voices to choose from and the power to choose?

Do these questions intrigue you? Does the scenario they describe appear attractive but not realistic? If your answer to the last two questions is yes, then you are at a crossroads. You are about to embark on a journey of transformation. I say this because I have walked this path and have changed my life beyond anything I could have possibly dreamed of. Thank you for allowing me to be your guide.

May LOVE and LIGHT always guide you on your path.

God Realization

Is religion a broken concept? It would be easy to substitute the word "God" for the word "religion", but that is not the question. God, even if it were broken, is so beyond our ability to comprehend, that we would never know if it were broken or not. As spiritual beings occupying a physical body, we are simply unable to ascertain the true nature of the Divine Presence, much less the source behind that presence. This is true even if we believe that our mission here on earth is to grow spiritually enough to become companions of and co-creators with God. At best, we can only perceive God working in our lives for our betterment and learn to believe in that presence. God's presence and intervention in our lives is seen retroactively, never predicted. If we could forecast God it would so severely diminish the entity we are forecasting to make the potential relationship almost worthless.

So back to the original question: Is religion a broken concept? I'm not going to spend a lot of time explaining why I am asking this question. You can find the reasons yourself in countless daily newspaper articles and on many news programs, which you can turn to for information on the status of the world we live in. The things we have done and continue to do in the name of God—and of God's perceived religion of choice and religion's most respected prophets—have nothing to do with that religion nor the teachings of those prophets.

Rather, these things done "in the name of God" reflect ego/self-will/shadow—and it is ego/self-will/shadow that creates religion. It is ego/self-will/shadow that sub-divides religion into multiple belief systems due to intolerance of minor points of doctrine. Likewise, it is ego/self-will/shadow that convinces the practitioner that other practices are heresy and must be eliminated at any cost.

The prophet Isaiah transmitted (in my opinion) a Divine directive regarding ceremonial practices. The King James Bible, The Book of the Prophet Isaiah, chapter 1, verses 10 – 17 reads as follows:

"Hear the word of the LORD, ye rulers of Sodom; give ear unto the law of our God, ye people of Gomorrah. To what purpose is the multitude of your sacrifices unto me? saith the LORD: I am full of the burnt offerings of rams, and the fat of fed beasts; and I delight not in the blood of bullocks, or of lambs, or of he goats. When ye come to appear before me, who hath required this at your hand, to tread my courts? Bring no more vain oblations; incense is an abomination unto me; the new moons and Sabbaths, the calling of assemblies, I cannot away with; it is iniquity, even the solemn meeting. Your new moons and your appointed feasts my soul hateth: they are a trouble unto me; I am weary to bear them. And when ye spread forth your hands, I will hide mine eyes from you: yea, when ye make many prayers, I will not hear: your hands are full of blood. Wash you, make you clean; put away the evil of your doings from before mine eyes; cease to do evil; Learn to do well; seek judgment, relieve the oppressed, judge the fatherless, plead for the widow."

We are not here to create ritual and dogma in the name of God or religion—we are here to be of service to the spiritual souls we meet on our journey. A wonderful Tao teaching states: "There is only one path and we are all walking it…. There are only two types of people on the path, those who are in front of us and those who are behind us." The teaching closes with: "When we meet someone ahead of us on the path, we are called upon to learn from them and when we meet someone behind us we are called upon to be compassionate and offer to teach."

I will answer the opening question—Is religion a broken concept—using a systemic perspective and—more importantly—I will provide an alternative, not a fix for, this broken theory. The present system has been around and entrenched far too long to be fixed.

Karl Marx has been famously quoted as saying: "Religion is the opium of the people." The complete quote per Wikipedia is: "Religion is the sigh of the oppressed creature, the heart of a heartless world, and the soul of soulless conditions. It is the opium of the people."

On that note, I will start with the question: "What is the definition of religion?" The origin of the word "religion", according to Oxford Dictionaries.com, is Middle English (originally in the sense "life under monastic vows"): from Old French, or from Latin religio(n-) "obligation, bond, reverence", perhaps based on Latin "religare" 'to bind'. Googling "define religion" yields the following information:

    a. the belief in and worship of a superhuman controlling power, especially a personal God or gods;

    b. a particular system of faith and worship;

    c. a pursuit or interest to which someone ascribes supreme importance.

Dictionary.com provides the following definitions:

    a. a set of beliefs concerning the cause, nature, and purpose of the universe, especially when considered as the creation of a superhuman agency or agencies, usually involving devotional and ritual observances, and often containing a moral code governing the conduct of human affairs;

    b. a specific fundamental set of beliefs and practices generally agreed upon by a number of persons or sects;

    c. the body of persons adhering to a particular set of beliefs and practices;

    d. the life or state of a monk, nun, etc.;

    e. the practice of religious beliefs; ritual observance of faith;

    f. something one believes in and follows devotedly; a point or matter of ethics or conscience.

However, defining religion doesn't tell us its purpose, because definitions only tell us what a word means, not how to go about demonstrating that word in the real world. So, I will state here that the purpose of religion is to take individuals and instruct them sufficiently so that they transcend the need for the very teachings and guidance they received in their training. At this point in their journey, individuals will be guided by their connection with Divine Consciousness.

The more the individual empowers their oneness, the more they unify their human self into their Divine self. Ultimately, with a focused and purposeful practice, the ego is transcended, leaving only the spirit. In the Vedic tradition, this is called *God Realization*. Wikipedia defines *God Realization*, in the words of the Indian guru Meher Baba, "As the highest state of consciousness and the goal and ultimate destiny of all souls in Creation. A soul that realizes God experiences God's infinite power, knowledge, and bliss continuously.... What keeps man from this state of consciousness is the ego, the identification with a false self. Ultimately the ego weakens through endless expression of itself in many lifetimes of experience, finally disappearing completely in full Self or *God Realization*...." According to Meher Baba "one gets *God Realization* at the hands of one Master, but for knowledge, which the Muslim Sufis call Irfan and the Hindu Sages Jnana, it may be necessary for him to approach more Masters than one."

A NON-QUANTIFIABLE PRODUCT

Why then are we, as a society, so driven by the ego/self-will/shadow instead of Spirit? Because our religions are failing in their mission. Perhaps one of the reasons that religion is a broken concept is because our religions do not honor their primary purpose: to teach and guide the individual practitioner to transcendence. As I see it, religion's splintered approach to pastoral guidance is at the root of this problem. How does a particular religious sect distinguish itself from a very similar religious sect? If the two sects were marketing a soda, for example, they could hold comparative taste tests. The soda with the most votes proves itself to be the better tasting soda. Obviously, religious sects do not have the ability to hold taste tests since the Divine Presence is a singular, non-quantifiable product.

So how does one sect separate itself and make itself a more desirable destination than another sect? By the number of practitioners. If my sect has ten practitioners and your sect has only five, then my sect is, by virtue of a larger head count, better than yours. So, in order for my sect to survive and be the more desirable destination, we have to do two things:

1. continue to add more new members than your sect does
2. not lose any existing members.

The best way to accomplish both requirements is to offer a better product. How can God become a better product? It can't. Therefore, we need to change the environment wherein members connect to God. We achieve this by:

1. building bigger and more lavish houses of worship, which creates the dynamic of diverting more and more resources towards the physical structure as opposed to using them to care for God's children;
2. hiring a more dynamic, charismatic leader/teacher, making the sect a cult of personality;
3. making the delivery of the theology more entertaining; for example, adding live musical accompaniment and/or creating programmed musical interludes.

Another by-product of this approach is that the focus of the sect becomes more about its survival as a sect than the spiritual growth and transcendence of the individual practitioners. In Taoism, we are taught that the greatest master is not the one with the most students. The greatest master is the one who produces the most masters. Somewhere along the way the Abrahamic traditions have lost this simple yet important concept.

The purpose and practice of religion conflict with each other, especially in the Abrahamic traditions. I'm singling out the Abrahamic religions because I find this inherent conflict is much more prevalent in these dogmas than in Eastern religions, which in my opinion are more philosophies then religions. I believe there are factors that create this dynamic. Ultimately, as Meher Baba states, ego is the primary factor in this conflict. If an individual can overcome their ego they will experience *God Realization* regardless of the practice they follow or the religion they observe.

THE CYCLE OF AGES

Are there factors that feed the Abrahamic ego that are not as prevalent or as strong in the Eastern religions? My answer is yes. If yes, then why are the Abrahamic traditions more plagued by these influences than the Eastern traditions? To find the answer to this question we need to look at the Vedic concept of "Yuga – The Cycle of Ages." A significant amount of information can be found on the Internet regarding this topic. For the purpose of simplicity, I am going to use as a reference, the book God Without Religion: Questioning Centuries of Accepted Truths by Sankara Saranam (© 2005). A two-part interview with the author can be found at http://churchoftheonegod.org/RadioShowListings.htm under the subject "God Without Religion".

Sankara puts forth the following interpretation of the "Cycle of Ages": There is an energy, a consciousness, at the center of the Milky Way galaxy that our Earth-contained solar system rotates around. This energy or consciousness is pure understanding of the workings of existence. As we get closer to this energy or consciousness on our galactic rotation, we gain knowledge and understanding. As we get further away from this energy or consciousness, we lose knowledge and understanding.

Sankara breaks this galactic journey down into ascending and descending segments. If we picture a circular clock, let's make twelve o'clock the zenith. Sankara identifies this point as the cusp between ascending and descending segments, identifying this as the year 11,501 BCE and designates this as the apex of the Gold Age. On the descend, the Gold Age covers 4,800 years, lasting until approximately 6,700 BCE. At this point the descending Silver Age begins and lasts 3,600 years until approximately 3,100 BCE. Then the descending Bronze Age begins and lasts 2,400 years until approximately 700 BCE. The next age, the bottom one encompassing six on the clock, is the Iron

Age. The Iron Age lasts 2,400 years, 1,200 years on the descend and 1,200 years on the ascend. The midpoint of the age is 500 CE. This is the point where the descent is completed and the ascent begins.

On the cycle upturn the Iron Age ends at approximately 700 CE. Then begins the ascending Bronze Age lasting until about 4,100 CE. At this point the ascending Silver Age begins and lasts for 3,600 years until approximately 7,700 CE, when the ascending Gold Age begins and continues 4,800 years until about 12,500 CE.

Sankara explains that our chakra system opens in conjunction with the age we live in. The Iron Age rules our bottom two chakras, the root and stomach. The Bronze Age rules our next two chakras, the solar plexus and the heart. The Silver Age rules our next two chakras, the throat and the third eye. The Gold Age rules the last chakra, the crown. Sankara instructs us that to grow past the chakras ruled by the age we find ourselves living in, we must practice a prescribed meditation. He outlines the meditative technique in detail in his book. Without this meditative practice, according to Sankara, we are stuck in the chakras ruled by the age we live in.

I introduced the "Cycle of Ages" because I believe it fully explains why the Abrahamic traditions and the Eastern religions/philosophies function as they do. To begin with allow me to list what I believe to be the major Eastern religions/philosophies: Hinduism (Vedanta), Taoism and Buddhism. The major Abrahamic religions are Judaism, Christianity and Islam.

THE EASTERN RELIGIONS/PHILOSOPHIES

Since the "Cycle of Ages" is Hindu in its origin and the roots of the Eastern religions/philosophies are older than the Abrahamic religions, I will start building my case from there. When we look at both Hinduism and Taoism we are challenged to pinpoint their origins. If we look to the production of their written texts, we have a more precise timeframe than if we look to the beginning of the oral tradition that the texts are based upon.

The Vedas (Sanskrit: knowledge, wisdom)—the oldest known scriptures in Hinduism, believed by some to be the first Divine texts—are the written result of a more ancient oral teaching. While the actual age of the oral teachings is unknown, most say the written text came into existence about 5,000 years ago. Many believe that these ancient oral teachings were a result of transmissions from The Creator to the Rishis, the Sages or Wise Men, who compiled the Vedas original oral tradition.

The Tao Te Ching (The Book of the Way) is traced to China circa 6th century BCE. The basis of the teachings contained in the book are believed to be founded in Shamanistic practices as old as 12,000 or so years ago, going as far back in time as over 2,000,0000 years ago. Using the 12,000-year timeframe, we find the roots of the Taoist practices situated close to the apex of the Gold Age, a time when we are very near, if not at, the optimal consciousness.

Buddhism traces its roots to Siddhartha Gautama, The Buddha (The Awakened One), and his teachings, circa 500 BCE. Although Buddhism is a relatively young religion (it might in fact qualify more as a philosophy than a religion due to its nontheistic teachings and practices) compared to its Eastern ancestors, Buddhism's underpinnings are rooted in the ancient understandings and teachings of the Vedas.

Another significant factor that distinguishes the Eastern religions/philosophies from the Western religions is that Eastern religions/philosophies heavily emphasize the practice of meditation. As Sankara stated, his meditation technique is essential to facilitate a practitioner's release from the influence of the age they live in. I suggest that any meditative practice will yield some liberating results, maybe not as liberating as Sankara's practice, but liberating nonetheless.

THE WESTERN RELIGIONS

The three Western religions all trace their origins back to Abraham, considered the first patriarch of Judaism, as given in the Book of Genesis, the first book of the Bible. According to Abrahamic

Tradition, Judaism is the first of the three Abrahamic religions. Next is Christianity, followed by Islam.

Abraham's date of birth is unknown. Based upon Biblical chronology Abraham is thought to have lived around 2,000 BCE. This places the birth of Judaism shortly thereafter, since Judaism is understood to begin with God's covenant with Abraham, which again takes place, according to Biblical chronology, when Abraham was approximately seventy-five years old. As we learned in the chronology of the "Cycle of Ages", the descending Bronze Age covers the years 3,100 BCE to 700 BCE. During this time period, we find the human species getting further away from the consciousness at the galactic center, nearing our most remote distance from that center. This means that whatever is created—brought into being during this Age—will reflect a minimum of the pure understanding of the workings of existence that is accessible at the center of the galaxy. This is not to say that Judaism wasn't ahead of its time, it was. However, compared with the Eastern religions/philosophies and their origins positioning in the "Cycle of Ages," Judaism doesn't reflect a high level of understanding of the workings of existence.

Regarding Christianity, it comes into existence, toward the end of the first century CE, as a minor sect of Judaism, following the death and resurrection of Jesus. This places the birth of Christianity approximately 400 years from the furthest point that our rotational journey takes us from the consciousness-raising galactic center point. What this means is that the lessons taught by Jesus, which are consistent with the wisdom revealed in the ancient Vedas, gets lost in their transmission because Jesus conveys his teachings in allegory and metaphor. Due to the lack of a consciousness-raising connection, Jesus' audience misinterprets the meaning of his teachings. Therefore, his audience lacks a basic understanding of them.

Islam comes into existence following the teachings of the transmissions Mohammed received in the early seventh century. This places the birth of Islam about 100-plus years nearer than the most remote section that our solar system takes on its galactic journey.

A secondary factor (an adjunct of the first factor and a reflection of their cyclic origins) is that the Abrahamic religions are rooted in the culture of a hunter-gatherer society. This is not to say that the hunting-gathering was taking place when and where these religions were born; but rather that the mindset—the culture—was so ingrained at the time of the birth of the Abrahamic religions that it was a defining influence. This mindset gives birth to conflict as not only a means of survival but also as a test of whose God is more powerful. This then creates a belief that there are multiple Gods that are masculine in nature, which leads to a belief that a warrior and his God gain influence and respect through conquest. Such a belief system promotes conflict as a desired way of life and stigmatizes the traits of mercy and compassion as weaknesses, which walks hand in hand with the idea that God needs to be appeased, whether by ritual and/or sacrifice, for one tribe to survive and/or overcome the other tribe. Ego feeds off this dynamic. Ego uses this dynamic to promote the concept that God is something outside of us as opposed to being within us. When we don't see God as being within us, we choose individualism over oneness and unity.

Jesus taught the principles of oneness and unity when he said, in The Gospel According to Saint Luke, (King James version, chapter 17, verses 20 and 21): "And when he was demanded of the Pharisees, when the kingdom of God should come, he answered them and said, The kingdom of God cometh not with observation: Neither shall they say, Lo here! or, lo there! for, behold, the kingdom of God is within you." Jesus continues this teaching from the same source (verses 27 and 28): "But I say unto you which hear, Love your enemies, do good to them which hate you, Bless them that curse you, and pray for them which despitefully use you." and finally in The Gospel According to Saint Matthew, the King James version, chapter 25, verse 40 "And the King shall answer and say unto them, "Verily I say unto you, Inasmuch as ye have done it unto one of the least of these my brethren, ye have done it unto me."

Ego also uses the built-in dynamic of conflict held sacred within the hunter-gatherer culture to not only devalue life, but also to elevate the male of the species over the female, creating the perception of false inequality on a spiritual plane of existence that is always in balance, as represented by the ancient Taoist yin/yang symbol . In addition, on a subliminal level, the hunter-gatherer mindset makes the deity in the image of the warrior as much as the warrior is made in the image of the deity. When this dynamic is prevalent, or even just present, the ethical moral ideals inherent in Divine Will become an inconvenient concept that is cast aside for personal gain, agenda promotion and collective affiliation. Furthermore, this identity association leads to a prejudicial evaluation of those whose skin color differs from the evaluator.

As stated earlier by both Mahatma Gandhi and Meher Baba, God's will for us is *God Realization*. God gave each of us Free Will as the primary teaching instrument to obtaining *God Realization* and will never, ever, interfere with our use of it. We are always allowed to choose Self Will over God's Will, regardless of the consequences. If God intervened in our lives, we would never learn how to use our Divine Power wisely.

The Creator does for its creations what they cannot do for themselves. What God will do is send us the prophet/teachers such as Krishna, Lao Tzu, Buddha, Abraham, Jesus and Mohammed. What God won't do is force us to embrace and practice the lessons. Each prophet/teacher God sends us is perfectly created for the message they are to teach and the message is delivered at the exact time the teachings will do the greatest good for the population it is intended to reach. These prophets/teachers are always rooted in the spiritual teachings of the people they are to inform, and the message is a course correction and advancement of the established teachings. Buddha arose from the Hindu/Taoist tradition, Jesus from the Judaic tradition and Mohammed from the Judeo/Christian tradition.

A WHOLE WORLD SPIRITUAL COURSE CORRECTION

With the creation and growth of the World Wide Web and the global reach of mass communications, the world we currently live in is rapidly advancing to a point where the artificial lines that designated the boundaries of countries, states and cities will become meaningless, perhaps even disappear, as exemplified by the European Union. If the Creator is an all-powerful and all-knowing entity, doesn't it make sense that it would not only be the source of this dynamic, but also would know how it could be best utilized to transmit a spiritual course correction, and an advancement, to all The Great Spirit's children, that would fit with the unified, boundless society that is being created? With that precognition, wouldn't it also make sense that The Creator would send us a prophet/teacher who would carry this message to a population in dire need of this transmission? It shouldn't be surprising, then, that this transmission—considering the source—would:

1. have a structure that allows for the message to be easily conveyed and implemented so that it could reach all of God's Creations, no matter where they are
2. it should not be surprising that this message would be compatible with the beliefs of the recipients, no matter what these beliefs are.

The structure I am putting forth and endorsing are the Twelve Steps and Twelve Traditions originated by Alcoholics Anonymous. I will be utilizing but adapting these two components to promote spiritual growth, not abstinence from any substance or behavior. My structure can be used by anyone and everyone. I've chosen the Twelve Steps and Traditions because of the versatility of their application.

THE OXFORD GROUP, ALCOHOLICS ANONYMOUS AND THE TWELVE STEPS AND TWELVE TRADITIONS

The Oxford Group and Alcoholics Anonymous

The fulfillment of the conditions stated in the previous paragraph start taking form in the year 1908 in, of all places, Philadelphia, PA, the City of Brotherly Love. I say of all places because where could be more appropriate to start up the next major course correction and advancement for the benefit of all humankind than the City of Brotherly Love.

What follows is a brief, extracted synopsis of the story of the Oxford Group, its connection to Alcoholics Anonymous (AA) and how the Twelve Steps and Twelve Traditions came into being. For the complete, unabridged story of the Oxford Group and its connection to AA please go to my source for the summation, the website http://silkworth.net/aahistory/oxford_group_connection.html.

In 1908 an individual named Frank Buchman started the "Church of the Good Shepherd" in Philadelphia. As "Church of the Good Shepherd" prospered, Frank created a hospice for young men. Frank then founded a settlement house project. Then Frank had a violent argument with his trustee committee because they cut his budget and food allotment. Frank resigned and went to Europe, ending up at a religious convention in Keswick, England. At the convention, Frank experienced a spiritual awakening. After making long distance amends for his behavior towards the trustees, Frank was guided to share his transformative experience at nearby Oxford University. He formed an evangelical group there among the student leaders and athletes.

Over the next twenty years this group grew into a fellowship with branches in Europe, Africa and Asia as well as South and North America. Its basic practices were based upon the Spiritual demonstrations of absolute surrender, guidance by the Holy Spirit, sharing, bringing about true fellowship, life-changing faith, and prayer. The Fellowship aspired to absolute standards of Love, Purity, Honesty, and Unselfishness. It adopted the name The Oxford Group, in 1928, and modeled itself after the First century Christian communities, and aggressively preached their message.

Two of the North American locations where the Oxford Group became established were Akron, Ohio and New York City, New York. It was in these two cities that the Oxford Group and the future founders of Alcoholics Anonymous (AA), Bill Wilson (Bill W) and Dr. Bob Smith (Dr. Bob), encountered the Oxford Group and each other.

The Oxford Groups took the newly sober alcoholics under their wing, teaching them their spiritual practices and hosting their early meetings.

The Oxford Group taught the following six basic principles:

1. We admitted we were licked.
2. We got honest with ourselves.
3. We talked it over with another person.
4. We made amends to those we had harmed.
5. We tried to carry this message to others with no thought of reward.
6. We prayed to whatever God we thought there was.

The Twelve Steps of AA

The evolution of the Oxford Group's six basic principles into the Twelve Steps can be found in "Where Did The 12 Steps Come From? A Fragment of History," an article written by Bill W. and published July 1953, in the AA Grapevine. Following is a brief, extracted synopsis of the above-mentioned evolution of the 12 Steps. For the unabridged story please go to my source for the summation that follows. The website can be found at http://www.barefootsworld.net/aa12stepsorigin.html

As the alcoholic population of the Oxford Group grew and as their focus became more and more about recovery from alcoholism, as opposed to the teachings of their parent group, the six basic Oxford Group principles evolved into the six principles of AA. At the beginning they became:

1. We admitted that we were powerless over alcohol.
2. We got honest with ourselves.
3. We got honest with another person, in confidence.
4. We made amends for harms done others.
5. We worked with other alcoholics without demand for prestige or money.
6. We prayed to God to help us to do these things as best we could.

In 1939, the idea arose that the AA program of abstinence and recovery should be more accurately and clearly stated. The ensuing debate in the fledgling AA fellowship produced the final, definitive version of the AA Twelve Steps. The agnostic contingent of the organization, after much heated discussion, convinced the fellowship that they must make the Steps easier for people like themselves who didn't have a specific, if any, religious conviction.

The final, definitive version of the AA Twelve Steps reads as follows;

1. We admitted we were powerless over alcohol—that our lives had become unmanageable.
2. Came to believe that a Power greater than ourselves could restore us to sanity.
3. Made a decision to turn our will and our lives over to the care of God as we understood Him.
4. Made a searching and fearless moral inventory of ourselves.
5. Admitted to God, to ourselves, and to another human being the exact nature of our wrongs.
6. Were entirely ready to have God remove all these defects of character.
7. Humbly asked Him to remove our shortcomings.
8. Made a list of all persons we had harmed, and became willing to make amends to them all.
9. Made direct amends to such people wherever possible, except when to do so would injure them or others.
10. Continued to take personal inventory, and when we were wrong, promptly admitted it.
11. Sought through prayer and meditation to improve our conscious contact with God as we understood Him, praying only for knowledge of His will for us and the power to carry that out.
12. Having had a spiritual awakening as the result of these steps, we tried to carry this message to other alcoholics, and to practice these principles in all our affairs.

The Twelve Traditions of AA

The need for and the origin of the Twelve Traditions of AA can be found in an article titled "Twelve Suggested Points of AA Tradition" by Bill W. (AA Grapevine, April 1946) The website can be accessed at http://www.barefootsworld.net/aatraditions-gv1946.html.

In this article, Bill W. states the reasons for the creation and adoption of the Twelve Traditions. Bill W. saw that with the publication of the book "Alcoholics Anonymous," the Fellowship's primary purpose had been fulfilled. He saw the Fellowship's next great challenge as being how they, as a fellowship, got along with one another as individuals and as groups, and how they collectively interacted with the outside world. As adjuncts to this issue, Bill W. saw the problem of the Fellowship's basic structure and its corresponding attitudes toward the subjects of leadership, money, and authority. He also saw that the future of the Fellowship could well depend on how the Fellowship dealt with things that were controversial and how it approached public relations. Ultimately, Bill W. came to realize that the destiny of the Fellowship would hinge on how the Fellowship dealt with all the above stated issues. Therefore, it was necessary to create Twelve Traditions.

The final, definitive version of the AA Twelve Traditions can be found in the Fourth Edition of the Big Book, the basic text for Alcoholics Anonymous and can be accessed online at http://www.aa.org/assets/en_US/en_bigbook_appendicei. The Twelve Traditions read as follows;

1. Our common welfare should come first; personal recovery depends upon AA unity.
2. For our group purpose there is but one ultimate authority—a loving God as He may express Himself in our group conscience. Our leaders are but trusted servants; they do not govern.
3. The only requirement for AA membership is a desire to stop drinking.
4. Each group should be autonomous except in matters affecting other groups or AA as a whole.

5. Each group has but one primary purpose—to carry its message to the alcoholic who still suffers.

6. An AA group ought never endorse, finance, or lend the AA name to any related facility or outside enterprise, lest problems of money, property, and prestige divert us from our primary purpose.

7. Every AA group ought to be fully self-supporting, declining outside contributions.

8. Alcoholics Anonymous 12th step work should remain forever non-professional, but our service centers may employ special workers.

9. AA, as such, ought never be organized; but we may create service boards or committees directly responsible to those they serve.

10. Alcoholics Anonymous has no opinion on outside issues; hence the AA name ought never be drawn into public controversy.

11. Our public relations policy is based on attraction rather than promotion; we need always to maintain personal anonymity at the level of press, radio, and films.

12. Anonymity is the spiritual foundation of all our traditions, ever reminding us to place principles before personalities.

THE GROWTH OF THE TWELVE STEPS

As the word spread regarding AA's successful utilization of the twelve steps to overcome alcoholism and the twelve traditions to function as a society, other fellowships started springing up, following AA's example, utilizing AA's twelve step/twelve tradition structures. Each fellowship was founded to deal with a specific obsessive/compulsive behavior that was impeding the participant's ability to lead a productive and fulfilling life. This utilization was accomplished by a simple rewording of the first step. Per Wikipedia (https://en.wikipedia.org/wiki/Twelve-step_program) there are over 200 Twelve Step self-help organizations with a collective worldwide membership of millions.

In order to understand why the twelve steps and twelve traditions have grown, in a space of some eighty plus years, from a small group of individuals attempting to overcome alcoholism to the huge numbers mentioned previously, I will turn to what are, in my opinion, two of the greatest minds of the twentieth century.

The first individual is Albert Einstein, who is credited with saying "No problem can be solved by the same kind of thinking that created it." (https://en.wikiquote.org/wiki/Talk:Albert_Einstein). Interpreting this statement, in the context of this thesis, translates it to mean that our problems are the result of listening to and acting on the thinking/voice of our ego/self-will/shadow. If we continue to listen to and act on what ego/self-will/shadow tells us we will never solve our problems nor resolve our issues, individually or collectively.

This brings us to my second individual, Dr. Carl Gustav Jung. As documented in AA's basic textbook, Alcoholics Anonymous Fourth Edition of the Big Book, page 27, (which can be accessed online at http://www.aa.org/assets/en_US/en_bigbook_chapt2.pdf), a dialog is credited to have taken place between Dr. Jung and an active alcoholic named Roland H. When Roland H. reportedly asked Dr. Jung if there was any sure way for an alcoholic to recover — truly recover, Dr. Jung is quoted as saying, "Yes, there is. Exceptions to cases such as yours have been occurring since early times. Here and there, once in a while, alcoholics have had what are called vital spiritual experiences. To me these are phenomena. They appear to be in the nature of huge emotional displacements and rearrangements. Ideas, emotions, and attitudes which were once the guiding forces of the lives of these men are suddenly cast to one side, and a completely new set of conceptions and motives begin to dominate them. In fact, I have been trying to produce some such emotional rearrangement within you. With many individuals the methods which I employed are successful, but I have never been successful with an alcoholic of your description."

What Dr. Jung is telling us is that, in order to solve our problems and resolve our issues, there is another voice we can listen to and act on—the voice of Spirit.

THE EVOLUTION AND UTILIZATION OF THE TWELVE STEPS

Utilizing Einstein's insight as to what will not solve our problems and Dr. Jung's advice as to what will solve our problems brings us to the core teaching of AA's Twelve Step program. AA has had more consistent success than Dr. Jung had with hardcore cases of alcoholism (As he stated: "With many individuals the methods which I employed are successful, but I have never been successful with an alcoholic of your description.") And I believe that can be attributed to a combining of the social factor—individuals of like mind and like kind working with each other and utilizing a common methodology (the Twelve Steps) who regularly convene in assemblies (the Twelve Traditions).

Each of the 200 or so variations of AA's twelve-step program work because of the simple, basic principles encompassed by the configuration of the twelve steps. A rudimentary overview shows us that the first step qualifies and quantifies Einstein's vision, while the remaining eleven steps guide us to Dr. Jung's solution. An in-depth spiritual explanation and application of each step will be provided later.

If each of the approximate 200 Twelve Step fellowships can achieve a level of success in addressing a specific obsessive/compulsive behavior–by rewording the first step to address that behavior and then using the healing properties of the remaining eleven steps—we can draw some important conclusions.

Firstly, is that there is a common root cause of all seemingly diverse behaviors being addressed. A reinterpretation of Einstein's understanding that "No problem can be solved by the same kind of thinking that created it" informs us that the common root cause, as demonstrated by the various applications of the twelve steps, is to be found in the fact that our ego/self-will/shadow guides our thinking. As Meher Baba teaches us, "What keeps man from this state of consciousness (*God Realization*) is the ego, the identification with a false self." We cannot solve our ego/self-will/shadow-created problems with our ego/self-will/shadow-created solutions. Why? Because God is One, God is Everything and ego/self-will/shadow guides us to a false belief of individuality, blocking the Divine understanding that

Jesus taught: "Inasmuch as ye have done it unto one of the least of these my brethren, ye have done it unto me." (King James Bible, The Gospel According to Saint Matthew, chapter 25, verse 40). The part, ego, can never be greater than the whole, God, but it can block and obscure the knowledge of Oneness.

The second conclusion we can come to is a reinterpretation of Dr. Jung's understanding, "Exceptions to cases such as yours have been occurring since early times. Here and there, once in a while, alcoholics have had what are called vital spiritual experiences." This guides us to the only solution available to us to overcome ego/self-will/shadow: following God's will for us. And the only way to consistently have knowledge of God's will for us, and then implement it, is to consistently work a spiritually empowering program. The ultimate destination of Dr. Jung's "vital spiritual experience" is demonstrated by the action of selfless service: honoring the whole of Divine Creation over the partial ego/self-will/shadow.

To reiterate the concept and reward of selfless service I turn to another one of the great individuals of the twentieth century, Albert Schweitzer. Schweitzer, a Nobel Peace Prize winning theologian, philosopher, and physician is quoted as saying http://www.quotationspage.com/quote/4120.html "I don't know what your destiny will be, but one thing I do know: the only ones among you who will be really happy are those who have sought and found how to serve."

THE EVOLUTION: WHERE CAN THE TWELVE STEPS LEAD US?

The evolutionary path of the Twelve Steps is in the deployment of the Steps to grow beyond a program that combats symptoms, to a program that combats the root cause of the symptoms. Why treat a manifestation of ego/self-will/shadow only to have another ego/self-will/shadow manifestation take its place? For example, using an AA participant, it would be replacing alcohol with gambling. The root cause of the alcohol dependence and the root cause of the gambling dependence are the same: an ego/self-will/shadow that tells the individual he/she is incapable of dealing with life on life's terms and the only recourse left is to run from life and from him/herself. That may sound futile, even ridiculous, but that is how ego/self-will/shadow compels its host. Whether it's alcohol, gambling, or any of the other 198 Twelve Step symptom – addressing fellowships, dealing with one dependence will only lead to another dependence.

The Twelve Steps are so Divinely structured that they are ideally constructed to deal with any behavior. Only the First Step deals with the ego/self-will/shadow manifestation. It helps the practitioner to stop from getting sicker by showing the practitioner that the dysfunction and wreckage of their obsessive/compulsive behavior are driven by the ego/self-will/shadow. The healing, which is spiritual in nature, starts with the Second Step and continues through the remainder of the Twelve Steps.

The Twelfth Step states, "Having had a spiritual awakening as the result of these steps, we tried to carry this message to other alcoholics, and to practice these principles in all our affairs." Why settle for an awakening, a discontinuation of one or maybe more obsessive/compulsive behaviors, when we can achieve *God Realization* employing a modified version of the same vehicle we are currently using?

If dealing only with manifestations created by the ego/self-will/shadow leads to dealing with different variations of those same manifestations, then let's work smarter, not harder. Let's create a new fellowship that will guide us to that *God Realization*. We can call it ESS (Ego/Self-will/Shadow) Anonymous (ESSA) or we can call Spirituality Anonymous (SA) or any other name that our Divine Presence guides us to.

THE UTILIZATION: HOW THE TWELVE STEPS AND TWELVE TRADITIONS CAN GET US TO GOD REALIZATION

Using the Twelve Step model gives us a proven program that reaches and awakens the Spirit. It does this by addressing and dealing with the dualistic nature of the human experience. By creating local groups that utilize the Twelve Steps and Twelve Traditions we can avoid the distractions and impediments that are plaguing most modern religions. As identified earlier in this book, these issues are:

1. Division of a religion over intolerance of minor points of theology.
2. Competition between practices that leads to accusations of heresy by one practice against another practice, with the only resolution being the destruction of the other practice at any cost.
3. Building bigger, more lavish houses of worship, which creates the dynamic of diverting more and more resources to the physical structure as opposed to using them to care for God's children.
4. Hiring a more dynamic, charismatic leader/teacher and making the sect a cult of personality.
5. Making a more entertaining delivery of the theology; for example, adding live musical accompaniment and/or creating programmed musical interludes.
6. The focus of the sect becomes more about their survival as a sect than the spiritual growth and transcendence of the individual practitioners.

Looking at the above six issues through the lenses of the Twelve Steps and the Twelve Traditions, we find the means to not only eliminate these obstacles from our path to *God Realization*, but also to return our Spiritual practices to the core exercises that promote our path to *God Realization* and give us the guidance that will get us there.

Issue 1 becomes a non-factor because the Twelve Step fellowships that are created have no theology at all. This happens because the fellowship's participants are not called upon to have a knowledge of their Deity's origin or nature, which is the basic definition of theology. The group participants, instead of discussing theology, discuss the manifestation of the Divine Presence in their lives and its will for them. Group participants support each other in dealing with the behavior identified in the First Step and in their quest for the *God Realization* promised in the Twelfth Step.

Issues 2 through 5 are rendered non-issues by the application of the Twelve Traditions. The adaptation and implementation of the Twelve Traditions will be covered later in this book.

Issue 6 becomes a non-factor because of the combined application of the Twelve Steps and the Twelve Traditions. The Steps teach the participants that their quest is an internal, not an external, one. The Traditions inform them that a connection to or relationship with any external entity is going to lead to disunity and dysfunction.

Now that we have the means to eliminate the factors that have created religions that are broken, what we can then create is a program that not only doesn't concern itself with anything external, but also guides the practitioner to the ultimate destination, *God Realization*.

The Twelve Steps: Reworded and Explained

With the identification of ego/self-will/shadow as our Step 1 focus and *God Realization* as the ultimate destination of Step 12, we can define this transformative journey through the steps in two ways. The first transformation is a journey from a false deity, ego/self-will/shadow, one that doesn't have our best interest and God-growth as its direct goal to a true deity, one that does have our best interest and direct God growth as its goal. The second transformation is a result of the first. We transform from an ego/self-will/shadow-focused being to one that sees the Divine oneness and connectivity of all beings and objects.

If we can accept these two directional definers then we can embrace the concept that each Step, as we implement it in our life, advances us on the path that brings us a little closer to *God Realization*. *God Realization* is an ongoing journey, not a destination. As long as we are breathing, the journey continues because ego/self-will/shadow is, as God is, ever present. This means we will constantly be challenged to maintain our state of *God Realization*. However, as we progress on the path the challenges will become easier to spot and the maintenance easier to implement.

To facilitate your journey towards *God Realization* I am providing a rewording and a spiritual explanation for each of the Twelve Steps, followed by a worksheet to help you implement and integrate each of the Twelve Steps into your daily life.

It has been my experience that when we engage in written exercises regarding each of the Twelve Steps it helps us to comprehend and implement their teachings in our lives. The following exercises are merely suggestions. You have free will. That means you can follow the suggestions exactly, modify them moderately, radically change them or ignore them completely. It's totally up to you and the guidance you receive from your Divine Self.

Please note that all the following definitions are, except where otherwise noted, sourced from Google.com.

For downloadable and printable worksheets for each Step please visit:

https://www.churchoftheonegod.org/assets/God-Realization_Step1.pdf

https://www.churchoftheonegod.org/assets/God-Realization_Step2.pdf

https://www.churchoftheonegod.org/assets/God-Realization_Step3.pdf

https://www.churchoftheonegod.org/assets/God-Realization_Step4.pdf

https://www.churchoftheonegod.org/assets/God-Realization_Step5.pdf

https://www.churchoftheonegod.org/assets/God-Realization_Step6.pdf

https://www.churchoftheonegod.org/assets/God-Realization_Step7.pdf

https://www.churchoftheonegod.org/assets/God-Realization_Step8.pdf

https://www.churchoftheonegod.org/assets/God-Realization_Step9.pdf

https://www.churchoftheonegod.org/assets/God-Realization_Step10.pdf

https://www.churchoftheonegod.org/assets/God-Realization_Step11.pdf

https://www.churchoftheonegod.org/assets/God-Realization_Step12.pdf

STEP ONE

"We admitted we were powerless to stop the impulses originated by ego/self-will/shadow, and that choosing to follow ego/self-will/shadow's direction for us, our lives are made unmanageable."

We open our journey through the Steps proclaiming two primary spiritual principles, unity and honesty, with the words "We admitted." The collective unity, "We", will continue to be re-emphasized in each of the remaining Steps. We can't and don't do this work, or embark on and partake of this journey, by ourselves. This journey is meant to guide us from the individuality of ego/self-will/shadow to the oneness of The Creator. Being alone, with the only voice we are listening to belonging to ego/self-will/shadow, can only lead us back to, and reinforce, what we are trying to transcend, ego/self-will/shadow. The collective, the "We," is not just being recommended—its presence is essential.

The principle of honesty—to admit the problem—is equally essential. If we can't admit that there is a problem, then one doesn't exist for us. We must admit it. It doesn't matter how someone else, regardless of their relationship to us, nor their status in the society we live in, sees us or defines us. If we don't admit to something, then it doesn't exist for us and if it doesn't exist, then nothing can be done about it.

The next phrase in this step, "we were powerless to stop," provides us with the first part of our admission. The "we" is restated, reminding us that we are not only doing this within a collective, but also that we aren't the only participant in the collective making this admission. This counteracts the ego/self-will/shadow's message that we are terminally unique and beyond redemption. The word "were" indicates a change of status. It isn't the present tense "are", it is the past tense. We have changed and can continue to change. This change has been facilitated by our becoming a member of the fellowship, and our exposure to the proof that individuals of like mind and like kind are overcoming the influence ego/self-will/shadow has asserted over them. "Powerless" implies an inability to affect any form of change. The "to stop" connects us to the problems created by the influence over our being that ego/self-will/shadow exerts.

Our fellowship has been formed to overcome a very specific problem stated in the next segment of this step: "impulses originated by ego/self-will/shadow." An impulse is "a sudden strong and unreflective urge or desire to act," The word "originated" guides us to the exact location of where our problem comes from, ego/self-will/shadow. We do not need a precise physical position to identify where our problem is situated. Our knowledge of its existence is enough.

The remainder of Step One pinpoints the problem. The impulse on its own is not the real problem. The real problem is stated clearly: "choosing to follow ego/self-will/shadow's direction for us our lives are made unmanageable." The impact on our being, both physical and spiritual, that is caused by following ego/self-will/shadow's directional guidance becomes our second admission. The impact is that our lives have been made "unmanageable." The word "unmanageable" means "difficult or impossible to manage, manipulate, or control." The guidance ego/self-will/shadow gives us is dysfunctional and the result of following dysfunctional guidance is a dysfunctional life.

The First Step helps us understand the source and nature of the pain and suffering in our lives. However, it doesn't provide us with any means of healing that pain or eradicating the suffering. It teaches us what not to do: Do not act on the impulses originating from ego/self-will/shadow. It teaches this by asking us to identify the energy/flavor/taste that comes with the impulses generated by ego/self-will/shadow. But the Step doesn't teach us what to do. Rather, it infers that we have power over our own actions, whether mental, emotional, physical or spiritual. We create our inner reality by the actions we choose to take or not take. Learning that there is a force that can guide us to actions that don't make our lives powerless and unmanageable is the antidote to the lessons taught by Step One. The process of learning and implementing that remedy starts with the Second Step and continues through the rest of the Steps.

By admitting that we create our own reality by the actions we choose to take and do not take, we gift ourselves with an extremely important lesson. That gift, that lesson, is the shattering of our victim stance. We are volunteers. We can choose other actions. We can choose other interpretations of the events we find ourselves in. Life is done for us, not to us. How this transformation comes into existence begins to be revealed with Step Two.

STEP ONE WORKSHEET

1. *Write a brief statement,* in your own words, describing what the above explanation of Step One has taught you.

2. On a sheet of paper create two columns. Work this Step by going from a listed impulse in column one to the feelings and effectiveness of acting on that impulse in column two. This allows you to connect on a more direct basis with your feelings and evaluation of the behavior that you are listing.

3. In the first column list the things that you can think of that:
   a. You attempt to control.
   b. You attempt to manipulate.
   c. You attempt to change.
   d. You react to with anger.
   e. You react to with frustration.
   f. You wish would be different (Expectations).

4. In the second column, alongside each item appearing in the first column, describe how you feel after you have engaged in the conduct listed and how effective each of your engagements were in the specified behavior. Also, work on becoming aware of the energetic and physiological shifts you go through when you engage in the conduct listed as opposed to when you are not engaged in that conduct.

STEP TWO

"We came to believe that a Power greater than ourselves could restore us to sanity."

Our healing/transformation starts here, with the Second Step. The Second Step is the step of hope, the step of open mindedness, the bridge from insanity to sanity. Just as in the First Step, the ever-present word "We" leads us off. What are we doing? We are arriving at a time and place we are accepting as being true and real. We arrive at this place due to the honest examination of our lives that we did in Step One. What we are being asked to accept as true and real is yet to be revealed. The remainder of the step will guide us to this belief.

The Second Step goes on to tell us what we are being asked to come to believe in: "a Power greater than ourselves." This phrase "a power greater than ourselves" is an extremely potent statement. When we substitute those shortcut words such as God or Higher Power or Spirit etcetera, we aren't doing justice to this highly descriptive, forceful phrase. When I was first introduced to Step Two this phrase was explained to me that "a power greater than ourselves" means "a power capable of accomplishing things that are beyond my ability to imagine and/or comprehend," not just something more powerful than myself. There are lots of people and things that are more powerful than myself, and they can do me great physical damage, but they are incapable of accomplishing feats beyond my ability to imagine and/or comprehend. In order to accomplish feats beyond my ability to imagine and/or comprehend wouldn't this entity then be all-powerful, all-knowing and ever present. Add to this the trait of being unconditionally loving, since no matter what the actions are that require intercession and/or intervention the outcomes are minimized to soften the impact while strong enough to give the necessary lesson.

The remainder of this Step informs us what this belief can do for us. It "could restore us to sanity". Please note that Step Two uses the word "could". It doesn't say will. The restoration is conditional. What Step Two is leading us to is that we need to do something. That, a belief, on its own, has no power. A belief, any belief, can drive our actions but it is not an action. The action the "could" is guiding us to is Step Three.

Also, Step Two doesn't state "eliminate the behavior addressed in Step One from our reality." It states, "restore us to sanity." The implication is clear: there is more to our insanity than the behavior addressed in Step One. That the insanity in our lives is the allowance of ego/self-will/shadow's will for us to be implemented in our lives.

Sometimes it is beneficial to define the opposite of a word to understand that word better. "Sanity" is one of those words. The following seven definitions of insanity proved most enlightening for me:

1. Doing the same thing repeatedly, expecting a different result.
2. Doing the same thing repeatedly knowing the result you will get.
3. Acting on first impulse.
4. Trying to fix what's broken inside of us with something outside of us. If we can accept this definition of insanity, then the yang to this yin is that there is nothing outside of us, short of a physical attack, that can damage us.
5. To willfully inflict harm on self or others.
6. To stop doing something despite the evidence that it is facilitating a successful outcome in our lives.
7. The ultimate demonstration of our insanity, an extension of the sixth definition, is our willing disconnection from that power that is greater than ourselves.

The linear progression of the Steps helps us to understand that in order to stop the ego/self-will/shadow from running/ruining our lives (as revealed in Step One), we must apply the Step Two teaching and allow a "power greater than ourselves" to guide us. How do we distinguish which voice we are allowing to guide us? By the energy/flavor/taste it's delivered with. This "power capable of accomplishing things that are beyond our ability to imagine and/or comprehend" has a will for us that has a distinctive energy/flavor/taste as opposed to the one generated by ego/self-will/shadow. Therefore, in the simplest of terms, we will define insanity as consciously taking an action that we determine originates in ego/self-will/shadow."

The more we meditate, the easier it becomes to recognize and capture the voice of a "a power capable of accomplishing things that are beyond our ability to imagine and/or comprehend". "A power capable of accomplishing things that are beyond our ability to imagine and/or comprehend" is always the first responder to any situation we may find ourselves in. Ego/self-will/shadow's voice always, without exception, responds second. There is a passage in the Bible, the King James Version, 3 Kings, chapter19, verses 11 and 12 that describes that first response beautifully. It reads as follows: "And he said, Go forth, and stand upon the mount before the LORD. And, behold, the LORD passed by, and a great and strong wind rent the mountains, and brake in pieces the rocks before the LORD; but the LORD was not in the wind: and after the wind an earthquake; but the LORD was not in the earthquake: And after the earthquake a fire; but the LORD was not in the fire: and after the fire a still small voice." That "still small voice" can be described as a knowing, an intuition, a gut reaction to just name a few. It doesn't say much. Basically, it will say "yes child" or "no child". It doesn't need to give lengthy explanations. Once the "still small voice" has finished the voice of ego/self-will/shadow is free to speak. It will rationalize, manipulate and justify any advice it offers up. It will try to confuse the listener by having it create lists of pros and cons or weigh factors out on some arbitrary scale. It will play to the listeners weaknesses. It will even at times try to pretend to be the voice of the First Responder. Its response will always be lengthy. It wants to put as much space/time between its response completion and the conclusion of the "still, small voice".

Step Two is where we transcend religion because we are not being told what to believe in; we are being instructed to "come to believe" based upon our own experiences and our interpretation of them. This important distinction makes this a Spiritual process and not a religious one. We are not being instructed to "come to believe" in an origin and nature of a power greater than ourselves, which is the definition of theology. We are not being told what to call this entity nor how and when to communicate with it. We are being instructed to "come to believe" in the presence of a power greater than ourselves in our lives and that it intervenes in our lives for our betterment. Unlike religion, which is theoretical, basically giving us a book and telling us to accept it as Divine Instruction even when we do not know the author or have any relationship to the time and place the narrative is set in. Our belief is experiential, our own interpretation of the events in our lives.

Based upon these interventions "we come to believe" that a power greater than ourselves loves us unconditionally. We also come to believe that our actions and experiences don't define us, they inform us, God defines us. This Unconditional Love is demonstrated in numerous ways, foremost of which are:

1. Non-judgment
2. Mercy
3. Grace

All of this works because of the Divine Law that two things are required to create or change our reality. First, we need to have a belief in order to take an action. There will never be any action we take that doesn't have a belief fueling it. Secondly, intention must be in place before we act. To fulfill this second requirement and satisfy the word "could" in the wording of this Step we must progress to Step Three.

One final point before we proceed on to Step Three. We are never, ever, done with Step Two. Based upon the definition of "a power greater than ourselves" meaning "a power capable of accomplishing things that are beyond our ability to imagine and/or comprehend," then how can all the potential situations we will face in our lives ever be revealed to us, and how can we fully know all the interventions of this power greater than ourselves in our lives? Richard Bach teaches us in "Illusions" "Here is a test to find whether your mission on earth is finished: If you're alive, it isn't."

The Second Step is the foundation of our healing/transformation. In order for our Spirit to continue to grow and mature Step Two must remain forever unfinished and fluid. The concept that "more shall be revealed" needs to be embraced unconditionally. No matter what episode of revelation we find ourselves experiencing, we must hold dear our beliefs that a power greater than ourselves is all-powerful, all-knowing, ever present and unconditionally loving. This means is that whatever we are experiencing is being done for us not to us. Also consider, if this entity is ever present are we not a part of that presence? In simple terms are we not, each and every one of us, God, just not God Almighty?

STEP TWO WORKSHEET

1. *Write a brief statement,* in your own words, describing what the explanation of Step Two has taught you.

2. Have there ever been times when, in spite of your best thinking, feelings and actions, the consequences weren't nearly as severe as they could have been?

3. What have you "come to believe" about "a power greater than ourselves"? Try to include in your answer the following:

4. Are there limits to its power? If so, what are they?

5. Does this power use its power for your benefit? If so, how and why?

6. Does this power communicate with you? If so, how and why?

7. Can you communicate with this power? If so, how and why?

8. What have you "come to believe" regarding the attributes and manifestations of this power? How do these beliefs manifest in your life?

9. What have you "come to believe" regarding the attributes and manifestations of this power when the situation involves more than just yourself?

10. Consider the following four questions and answers. Write a brief statement regarding what they collectively teach you about Step Two.

    Q 10-1: What if there isn't a power greater than ourselves and you do not believe?

    A 10-1: There is nothing, you have nothing, and you lose nothing.

    Q 10-2: What if there isn't a power greater than ourselves, and you do believe?

    A 10-2: Your perceptions are your reality. At least you will get some comfort in believing in something.

    Q 10-3: What if there is a power greater than ourselves and you do believe?

    A 10-3: You win. Your belief has a foundation.

    Q 10-4 What if there is a power greater than ourselves and you do not believe?

    A 10-4: You're up the creek without a paddle!

STEP THREE

"We made a decision to turn our will and our life over to the care of a power greater than ourselves as we understood that power greater than ourselves."

In the First Step, we are shown what happens to our lives if we allow ego/self-will/shadow to guide us in the use of the awesome power to create our own reality that a power greater than ourselves has endowed us with. The power to create our own reality, as guided by ego/self-will/shadow, creates unmanageability and insanity! In the Second Step, we are introduced to what bestows this power, and we are shown that it could guide us out of the state of unmanageability and insanity we placed ourselves in.

The Third Step is where the beliefs we have come to in Step Two are turned into action. In the King James Bible, The Epistle of Paul the Apostle to James (chapter 2, verse 17), we can find this relationship between belief and action clearly stated: "Even so faith, if it hath not works, is dead, being alone."

"We" leads us off, again. What are we being guided to do? To make a decision and commit to a course of action. We are not being asked to sign a contract and file it in a drawer. Life is an ongoing, continuous series of lessons. As stated in Step Two and worthy of repetition here, Richard Bach instructs us in "Illusions" "Here is a test to find whether your mission on earth is finished: If you're alive, it isn't." These lessons, simply expressed, are our Karma, our mission. Karma is a system that manifests cause and effect. Karma's function is to get us to a crossroad. At that point Karma ceases as an influence and free will kicks in. Each lesson/crossroad requires us to make a decision as to how we react to what is being placed in front of us. We have free will to choose. There are only two voices to choose from. The voice of ego/self-will/shadow, the voice that gives us a harsh lesson, as revealed in the First Step, or the voice of Spirit that gives us a gentle lesson, as revealed in the Second Step. Which voice guides our actions determines how we deal with and what we take away from our experiences.

At this point it is important to explain the dynamic that produces the two voices. It will also explain, in a deeper, clearer sense, the phrase in Step Two "whatever we are experiencing is being done for us not to us." In Step Two we have come to believe, accepted as being true and real, that this entity is all-powerful, all-knowing, ever present and unconditionally loving. If these four factors are always in force, ever present, then, can there ever be anything we experience that doesn't originate from a condition of unconditional love? If everything we experience originates in a state of unconditional love and whose sole intention is to facilitate our Spiritual growth, then can anything we ever experience not be done for us as opposed to us. We are being given the choice, Step Three, between the voice that provides us with a gentle lesson, met in Step Two, and the voice that provides us with a harsh lesson, met in Step One. The purpose of the lesson, Karma, is for us to grow Spiritually. Whether we have a gentle lesson or a harsh one is purely our choice. The lesson is what matters.

Step Three goes on to teach us how important a decision we are being asked to make. It is explained that "To turn our will and our lives over to...." means that our will is the power behind our actions and our life is the result of those actions. To avoid acting insanely we need to find the right guidance for the choices we make in using the Divine power we possess. We are directed to that Power and the guidance it can provide with the remainder of this Step.

Before we proceed, it is important to note here that we are being guided specifically to turn our will and our lives over, not to turn a situation over. The situation will always be exactly as it's supposed to be. It's our inability to accept that situation, and not the situation itself, that is creating our unmanageability. Remember, we have come to believe that a power greater than ourselves is all-knowing, all-powerful, ever present and unconditionally loving. Given these parameters can anything we ever experience not be exactly as it is supposed to be? Let us take that statement further—we are both the teacher, determining what lesson needs to be addressed, and the student, determining how much we want to engage in the lesson. Therefore, can we ever give ourselves a lesson we don't need, that we don't possess the tools required to engage in the task at hand and aren't prepared to successfully complete? The only reason we will ever not successfully complete a lesson is because we have been guided by the voice of the harsh lesson, the voice of ego/self-will/shadow.

If a situation is always exactly as it's supposed to be and it's only our inability to accept that situation that is creating our perception of a problem, then can we ever not be exactly where we are supposed to be? If you ever hear the internal statement that you are not where you are supposed to be you are listening to the voice of ego/self-will/shadow.

Another statement that is a favorite of ego/self-will/shadow is that we should have done something better than we did. We are always our most perfect demonstration. We may demonstrate differently in a similar situation at another time, however at any given time we are always our most perfect demonstration. We are spiritual beings in a physical body. The Divine Wisdom for this dynamic is to teach us the ultimate lesson of detachment, care for the body without allowing it to supplant God in our lives. The human body has three sub-bodies; the physical, the mental and the emotional. They are independent of each other but are connected. How well each body is functioning and how clear the transmission and reception of information is are factors in how the individual responds to any given situation. As we advance on our spiritual journey the influence of the three will diminish.

The remainder of this Step is our directive as to what we are turning our will and our lives over to. It reads "the care of God as we understood God." The word "care" links us back to the Second Step, in that it invokes the belief we have come to that "a power greater than ourselves" loves us unconditionally. Without this reminder, we may be at a loss as to why we are turning over anything, much less our will and our lives. Keep in mind, we have come to believe that our life experiences are being done for us not to us.

The name "God" is used twice in Step Three and will appear again in a number of the remaining Steps. "God" is used generically and does not imply an endorsement of any religion, theology, belief system or spiritual practice. It is being used because of the near universality of the word. If the word "God" offends you or makes you uncomfortable or you just don't resonate with it, then feel free to substitute whatever word or name or descriptive that works for you.

The final word left to break down is "understood." The usage of the past tense of the verb "understand" is employed here intentionally as a reminder that the decision we are making is the demonstration of the beliefs we have come to in the Second Step. We can never, ever, understand God. By the very nature of our definition of "a power greater than ourselves" that would be contradictory. If you have a Deity that you understand then you are boxing it in and placing non-existent limitations on it. Discard it and start over. As the Tao Te Ching, as translated by J. Legge, (first chapter, first verse), teaches us: "The Tao that can be trodden is not the enduring and unchanging Tao. The name that can be named is not the enduring and unchanging name."

There is a reverse side to the teaching presented in this Third Step. That is, whatever we turn our will and our lives over to becomes our de facto God. For example, let's say that we have a moral/intuitive/instinctive sense not to participate in a particular venture, such as lying for a good friend, but we allow ourselves to be swayed to partake in the lie because we are concerned with the relationship ramifications if we do not. We are not talking about compromise here; we are talking about giving in to look good and be accepted. In that very instance that we acted contrary to our moral/intuitive/instinctive sense, the recipient of our compromise has become our God.

There are only two wills in life: "God's Will" and the one originating from ego/self-will/shadow. We have all been given Free Will, which allows us to choose which voice we are going to act behind. Free Will does not, on its own, provide us with a direction or course of action. Therefore, Free Will has no energy/flavor/taste of its own. God's Will and the will of ego/self-will/shadow each have their own distinctive energy/flavor/taste. This difference facilitates our ability to choose between the two wills and their opposing directions for us. Simply put, we determine which action reflects the voice of the gentle lesson deity we have come to believe in, and which action comes with an attached harsh lesson and act accordingly.

On the following several pages, reproduced from "God Is" "Book 1 of the God Trilogy" are the three diagrams visualizing how Free Will interacts with ego/self-will/shadow and God's Will.

Shown first is the diagram of a neutral Free Will. Life presents a stimulus and both Spirit and ego/self-will/shadow interpret the stimulus and suggest a course of action to Free Will. Free Will makes a determination as to a response choosing either ego/self-will/shadow's or God's Will recommendation or some combination of both. Free Will sends the determination to Mind which then generates Action based upon the determination.

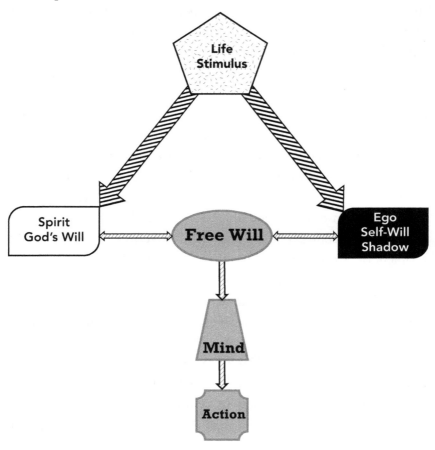

The more Free Will chooses ego/self-will/shadow the harder it becomes to choose Spirit. Harder doesn't mean impossible. To change it requires us to meditate, pray and stay in the moment. Doing this will change the coloring from dark to light, as pictured below.

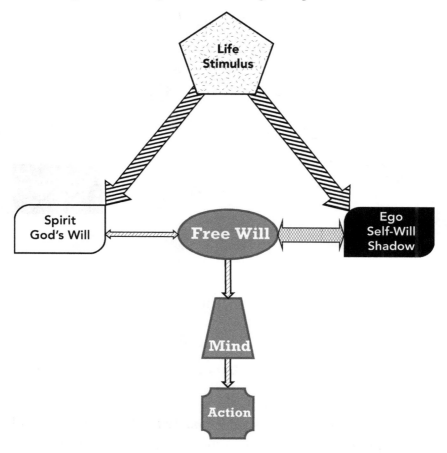

When we choose ego/self-will/shadow regularly our Free Will becomes colored with that determination, as pictured below.

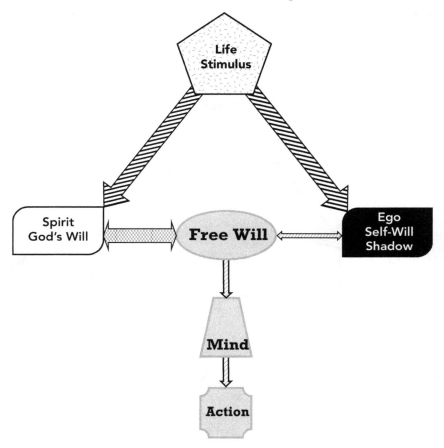

In "God Is", "Book 1 of the God Trilogy", I discuss in detail some of the lessons imparted to me by my Beloved Teacher, Maulana Zainulabedin-Kazmi. One of those lessons was that "God created Angels to serve God. They have no Free Will." Maulana goes on to further teach "God created humans to serve Humans". That service is the ultimate demonstration of God's Will, the proof of our Spiritual awakening which will be discussed in greater detail in Step 12.

God will never do for us what we can do for ourselves. God will only do for us what we cannot do for ourselves. God gave us Free Will so we can learn from our choices. God will never interfere with our Free Will. God will, to the extent we allow it, intervene to save us from the full ramifications that our Free Will choice of ego/self-will/ shadow guidance has brought upon us. God will never, ever, override our Free Will choices. There would be no point to bestowing Free Will on us for God to override it when we are acting behind the voice that gives us harsh lessons. How would we learn? How would God's intervention facilitate our Spiritual growth?

In the paragraph above I specifically used the phrase, "to the extent we allow it", when referring to God's intervening to save us from the full ramifications that our Free Will choice of ego/self-will/shadow guidance has brought upon us. This wording reflects our relationship with and to an Unconditionally Loving Deity. Saving us from the full ramifications that our ego/self-will/shadow chooses is Grace.

Grace is our birthright, we don't have to earn it, we have to stop blocking Grace. If Grace needed to be earned, we would not be dealing with an Unconditionally Loving Deity. We block Grace by surrounding our being with a shield. This shield is created when we choose ego/self-will/shadow to guide us as opposed to God's Will. The more we choose ego/self-will/shadow as our guide the stronger the shield becomes. There will come a point when there will be such a lack of penetrability to the extent that God will not violate our Free Will choice with its Grace. Conversely, we make the shield more penetrable, allowing more Grace in, each time we choose God's Will instead of ego/self-will/shadow.

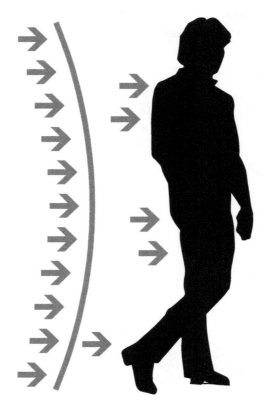

The more we choose to follow the guidance of the Divine, the easier our lessons become. The more we choose the harsh lesson, listening to the voice of ego/self-will/shadow, the harsher our lesson becomes. Gentle or harsh, we are still experiencing a lesson we chose to experience at a level of severity we have also chosen.

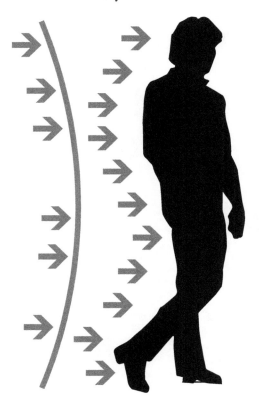

Finally, in its most comprehensive context, the term "God's Will for us" can be very far-reaching internally. If we are "coming to believe that a power greater than ourselves" is unconditionally loving and we are striving to "turn our will and our lives over" to that power's guidance, then are we not being asked to be unconditionally loving, in all of its manifestations, of ourselves and others?

STEP THREE WORKSHEET

1. *Write a brief statement,* in your own words, describing what the above explanation of Step Three has taught you.
2. How does one "turn our will and our life over"?
3. What is the difference between your will and God's will?
4. How can you utilize Step Three to increase your self-worth?
5. How can Step Three help you forgive yourself and others?

STEP FOUR

"We made a searching and fearless moral inventory of ourselves."

With the cumulative information amassed during our working of the first three Steps, we have been informed of the guidance of our actions Step Three instructs us to follow, choosing God's Will as our guide as opposed to allowing ego/self-will/shadow to be our guide. This leads us to the question: "What is God's will for us?" In the simplest of terms, God's Will for us is to Spiritually sustain our connection to the Divine Presence regardless of the external conditions we are presented with. God's Will for us is to be at peace, to walk through our life with serenity, dignity and grace. How we can implement this guidance is the function of Steps Four through Seven. These four Steps will begin to answer the question "What is God's will for us?"

We, in Step Four, as a part of the collective, are being directed to accomplish this by doing a searching and fearless moral inventory of ourselves. That means we are being asked to make as complete a list as we can of the numerous applications of the demonstration of unconditional love that we want to make. We are being asked to "do unto others as God has done unto us."

Who we are guided to do a searching and fearless inventory of is made abundantly clear by the final word in this Step, "ourselves." We are all called upon to do this Step for ourselves and not for others or for their approval of us. However, as part of the "we" we are called upon to support others in their process of working this Step.

The concept of "making a searching and fearless moral inventory"—making a complete list—presents us with a daunting task if we are going to list every moral, and all the situations, that could create a permutation of that definition and its application. That exercise would only lead us to frustration, not only in creating that list, but also in implementing it as well. However, that isn't what the previous Steps have led us to. Remember, we are being guided to recognize the distinctiveness between the energy/flavor/taste of the two wills. As our ability to distinguish between the two wills grows, our ability to make determinations that will move us towards the Light as opposed to away from the Light will grow also. This Step provides us with the guidance and opportunity to master the technique of ascertaining which voice we are listening to, and what voice we are about to act on. The recognition of the distinctive energy/flavor/taste of God's Will that the working of Step Four leads us to is, in a sense, the answer to the question Step Three presents: What does "turning our will and our life over" mean?

Step Four Worksheet

Write a brief statement, in your own words, describing what the above explanation of Step Four has taught you.

Step Four requires us to make "a searching and fearless moral inventory of ourselves." The following 16-character traits will help you to define and recognize your God-affirming beliefs. As your God-affirming beliefs are defined and recognized, be aware of the shift in the experience of your energy/flavor/taste sensation. Recognizing this is a fundamental tool in our Spiritual growth.

This process of defining your God-affirming beliefs will provide you with a basic awareness of the Divine compass you possess. You will need this compass to guide your actions when you have the manifestations of ego/self-will/shadow attempting to assert itself in your life.

After each trait is defined you will be asked to list both examples of your belief-conflicting behavior as well as your belief-agreeing behavior. This will help you to further recognize the distinctive energy/flavor/taste of God's will for you as opposed to ego/self-will/shadow's will for you. The continued development of your Divine compass is essential to the fulfillment of the *God Realization* process.

Take your time. Go at pace you're comfortable with. The 16 traits can be done in any order you want to do them in. If this feels overwhelming at any time, review your work on Step Three, particularly how this Step can help you find self-worth and forgive yourself.

Trait 1: Acceptance of Imperfection

God-affirming belief: Are you able to accept imperfection in yourself and others, or do you find yourself trying to "improve" through a critical attitude? What do you believe about the need for acceptance of imperfection?

Belief-conflicting behavior: List behaviors in which you desired perfection and were critical of yourself or others.

Belief-agreeing behavior: List behaviors in which you were tolerant of yourself or others and could accept.

Trait 2: Accomplishing

God-affirming belief: What do you believe about the importance of accomplishing the tasks that you set out to do within a reasonable length of time? How does putting it off affect you?

Belief-conflicting behavior: List behaviors in which you procrastinated.

Belief-agreeing behavior: List behaviors in which you accomplished what you set out to do within a reasonable length of time.

Trait 3: Anger

God-affirming belief: Write a statement of what you believe about the expression of anger. Include as a part of this statement your understanding of the origin of resentments. What have been your main resentments?

Belief-conflicting behavior: List how your way of dealing with anger has conflicted with what you currently believe. The examples may be times that you dealt with anger in a destructive manner or resentments that you have held because of another person's behavior.

Belief-agreeing behavior: List how you have dealt with anger according to what you currently believe.

Trait 4: Attitude About Self In Relation To Others

God-affirming belief: How do you see yourself in terms of the attitudes of self-pity and gratitude?

1. Do you find yourself feeling like a victim wallowing in self-pity at any time?
2. Does your attitude reflect gratitude?
3. Why is it important to feel grateful?
4. To whom do you feel grateful?

Belief-conflicting behavior: List incidents in which you were trapped by feelings of self-pity.

Belief-agreeing behavior: List incidents in which you were grateful and acted on that gratitude.

Trait 5: Attitude Towards Self

God-affirming belief: What has your attitude toward yourself been in the past? Are there things about yourself that you have found difficult to accept which led to feelings of self-hate? These things may include your appearance, a personal limitation, something about the way you are, or even something that you did or that happened to you for which you dislike yourself. Why is it important to love and accept yourself?

Belief-conflicting behavior: List behaviors in which you experienced self-hate.

Belief-agreeing behavior: List behaviors in which you loved and accepted yourself as you are.

Trait 6: Care Towards Others

God-affirming belief: Why is it important to care for others? What does it mean to care for another person?

Belief – conflicting behavior: List behaviors in which you have been indifferent and uncaring toward another person.

Belief-agreeing behavior: List behaviors in which you have shown care for someone else.

Trait 7: Centeredness

God-affirming belief: How has self-centeredness (selfishness) affected you? Write a statement of what you believe about the importance of finding another center for your life. What is your center now?

Belief-conflicting behavior: List examples of how your self-centeredness has hurt someone in the past.

Belief-agreeing behavior: List examples of how your "new center" can help you control your behavior.

Trait 8: Comparing

God-affirming belief: What do you believe about the process of comparing yourself to others? What does this process do to your contentment? How does envy and jealousy arise out of comparisons?

Belief-conflicting behavior: List examples of behavior in which the process of comparing led you into feelings of envy and jealousy.

Belief-agreeing behavior: List examples of behavior in which you were able to feel contentment by not comparing to the point where you got trapped into feeling envy and jealousy.

Trait 9: Control

God-affirming belief: Why is it important to let go and not try to control other people? What feelings come from attempts to control?

Belief-conflicting behavior: List examples of behavior in which you have tried to control someone else in a way that was damaging to yourself or to the other person.

Belief-agreeing behavior: List examples of behavior in which you "let go" and did not try to control.

Trait 10: Faith and Courage

God-affirming belief: Write a statement in which you define faith and courage. How are faith and courage a part of your life now? Why are they important to you? Are you currently making decisions based on your faith and courage?

Belief-conflicting behavior: List examples of your behavior in which fear has controlled what you did.

Belief-agreeing behavior: List examples of your behavior in which faith and courage have controlled what you did.

Trait 11: Freedom From Guilt Feelings

God-affirming belief: Guilt feelings come from doing something that goes against your values or beliefs. You might have guilt feelings about stealing, lying, cheating, hurting someone, destroying something, being unfaithful, etc. What have you learned about the importance of dealing with guilt feelings?

Belief-conflicting behavior: List examples of behavior about which you have felt guilt, especially situations that have not been discussed, where the guilt feelings still exist.

Belief-agreeing behavior: List examples of how you have found freedom from guilt by sharing what you feel guilty about with someone else.

Trait 12: Grief Process

God-affirming belief: What significant losses (death, divorce, broken relationships, etc.) have you experienced in your life? Now, how do you feel about each of these losses? Could you accept them or do feelings about them continue to affect your serenity?

Belief-conflicting behavior: List examples of behavior in which you tried to avoid facing a loss.

Belief-agreeing behavior: List examples of your behavior in which you have allowed yourself to experience grief over a loss.

Trait 13: Honesty

God-affirming belief: What are your current beliefs about the importance of honesty in your life? Why do you need to be honest?

Belief-conflicting behavior: Dishonesty comes in many forms. Included are such things as hiding, making alibis, thinking dishonesty (rationalizing, justifying), telling half-truths, being phony, lying, minimizing, being a people-pleaser, conning, and breaking promises. List examples for all the different forms of dishonesty mentioned.

Belief-agreeing behavior: List examples of behavior in which you were honest.

Trait 14: Responsibility

God-affirming belief: Write a statement of your belief about the importance of personal responsibility. What does it mean to be irresponsible? How is blaming related to being irresponsible?

Belief-conflicting behavior: List examples of how your past behavior has conflicted with your belief about the need to be responsible. List occasions in which you were irresponsible.

Belief-agreeing behavior: List examples of how you behaved according to your belief about the importance of personal responsibility.

Trait 15: Self-Esteem

God-affirming belief: Write a statement of your beliefs about how to achieve self-esteem without falsely trying to place yourself above other people. Include why self-esteem is important for you.

Belief-conflicting behavior: List examples of how you have tried to achieve self-esteem by placing yourself above others (grandiosity, false pride).

Belief-agreeing behavior: List examples of how you have achieved self-esteem by doing what you currently believe in.

Trait 16: Sexuality

God-affirming belief: What is your belief about the role of sexuality in your life? Include as a part of this statement what you believe about the role of sexuality in your relationships.

Belief-conflicting behavior: List examples of how your past behavior in the area of sexuality has conflicted with what you currently believe.

Belief-agreeing behavior: List examples of how your behavior in the area of sexuality has agreed with what you currently believe.

STEP FIVE

"We admitted to God, to ourselves, and to another human being the exact nature of our lessons."

Just as Step Two requires us to take action in Step Three, so does Step Four require us to take action which are Steps Five, Six and Seven. We must walk our talk, or our talk has no meaning. We start with Step Five, an admittance. With this admittance we are committing ourselves to the implementation of the inventory we took. The term "exact nature of our lessons" calls upon us to not be imprecise or inexact in any way, shape or form about the lessons we are committing to.

Where Step Five is steering us is to pronounce without hesitation what we are teaching ourselves regarding our ability to ascertain which of the two wills in our day-to-day life we are allowing to guide us. We are being called upon, admitting, to be vigorously open and honest about what we intend to do with regard to the implementation of the searching and fearless moral inventory we created in Step Four. Our admittance is being made firstly "to God," as a commitment to our spiritual growth. Our admittance "to ourselves" is setting the intention to do what is required, in the areas it is required in, and to honor our commitment "to God." Admitting "to another human being" enables us to have human accountability for the execution of our inventory.

There is another gift that this Step provides us with. It prioritizes our relationships for us. Our most important relationship is with "God." Our next important relationship is with "ourselves." The last and least significant of our relationships is with "another human being." The lack of a specific identity for that other human being is significant. It doesn't single out any one human relationship over all the others. "Another human being" teaches us that all human beings are equal, regardless of their earthly status.

The lesson we take away from this sequencing of the Step's wording is that thinking of "ourselves" or "another human being" as the most significant presence in our lives, or that "another human being" is a more significant presence than "ourselves," will divert us from the path we are walking. It is essential to maintain the sequence as presented by this Step if the practitioner desires to experience *God Realization*. We cannot become God Realized when we create false Gods in our lives or minimize our importance on this journey.

STEP FIVE WORKSHEET

Write a brief statement, in your own words, describing what the above explanation of Step Five has taught you.

STEP SIX

"We are entirely ready to have God inspire and empower us to eliminate our ego/self-will/shadow generated thoughts."

In Step Four we made a searching and fearless moral inventory of ourselves with the intent of teaching ourselves how to more easily distinguish what voice we are listening to and what voice our actions are being guided by. In Step Five we committed to God, to ourselves and to another human being the intention to be in God's will to the best of our ability. Step Six gives us the remedy to apply when we find ourselves immersed in ego/self-will/shadow originated thoughts.

Ego/self-will/shadow never rests, never abandons its mission. We need to be prepared to spiritually re-center ourselves at a moment's awareness. Recall, (I promise for the last time) Richard Bach's teaching from his book "Illusions" as quoted in the Step Two section "Here is a test to find whether your mission on earth is finished: If you're alive, it isn't." We strive to intervene on ourselves before our thoughts become actions. In Step Six we are given the tool to accomplish this task.

In plain language, this Step guides us to a Spiritual action, turning our will and our lives over to the care of God, through meditation, prayer and/or a statement of spiritual intention that will remind us of and restore us to the peace of being in God's will.

STEP SIX WORKSHEET

1. *Write a brief statement,* in your own words, describing what the above explanation of Step Six has taught you.
2. How will you know if you are entirely ready?
3. How will you determine if something is an ego/self-will/shadow – generated thought?
4. What will happen if you want to hold onto an ego/self-will/shadow – generated thought or you only want to partially remove an ego/self-will/shadow generated thought?
5. How does God inspire and empower us to eliminate ego/self-will/shadow generated thought?
6. What will the ego/self-will/shadow generated thoughts be replaced with?

STEP SEVEN

"With humility we asked God to inspire and empower us to redirect our actions that are being guided by ego/self-will/shadow."

There will be times during our journey, because we are never, ever going to do these lessons perfectly, where we will not recognize an ego/self-will/shadow generated thought stimulating us to action. Once we are aware that we are acting out in the throes of ego/self-will/shadow generated thought we have Step Seven to return us to our intended path, unity with God's will for us and the serenity that it brings. Step Seven uses the word humility. We can never be in God's Will if we are redirecting ourselves with arrogance. Arrogance will want us to approach God with shame and/or remorse. Shame and/or remorse are tools of ego/self-will/shadow. Humility is not thinking less of oneself, it is thinking of oneself less. Remember God doesn't and hasn't judged you (see Step Two) so don't judge yourself (Step Three).

As with Step Six, Step Seven, in straight forward language, guides us to a similar action, through meditation, prayer and/or a statement of spiritual intention that will remind us of and restore us to the peace of being in God's will and the serenity that being centered in God's will brings. The only difference is that Step Six is about dealing with a thought while Step Seven is about dealing with an action. Since our actions are more entrenched in the physical world than our thoughts, we will require a stronger response in Step Seven than we did in Step Six.

STEP SEVEN WORKSHEET

1. *Write a brief statement,* in your own words, describing what the above explanation of Step Seven has taught you.
2. How will you ask God to inspire and empower you to redirect your actions that are being guided by ego/self-will/shadow?
3. How will God inspire and empower you to redirect your actions that are being guided by ego/self-will/shadow?
4. How will you know if you have been inspired and empowered?

STEP EIGHT

"We will make a list of all individuals we have had a damaging effect on during acting out under the influence of ego/self-will/shadow and become willing to make appropriate amends to them all."

The Steps are sequenced intentionally. Step One starts off by introducing us to the nature of the problem in our life, listening to and acting on ego/self-will/shadow's direction for us. Steps Two and Three direct us to the solution to that problem, identifying and then allowing a Power greater than ourselves to guide us. Steps Four, Five, Six and Seven show us how that problem, listening to and acting on ego/self-will/shadow's direction, has previously manifested in our lives. These four Steps also give us the tools we need to counteract the potential problems brought on by the reemergence of that voice in our day to day lives. We do this by identifying and then allowing a Power greater than ourselves to guide us. Upon the completion of Step Seven, we are armed with the tools necessary to keep ourselves in reasonable check regarding what voice we are listening to and acting on.

We are now ready to look at how our actions, under the influence of ego/self-will/shadow, have had a significant detrimental impact on others in our life. We do this by making a list of all individuals we have had a damaging effect on. We are guided very precisely in identifying those we qualified for inclusion on this list, those "we have had a damaging effect on." How we define the term "a damaging effect on" is of critical importance. Ego/self-will/shadow will have us believe that we are responsible for damage that isn't damage or isn't a result of our actions. That is why we must work these Steps with an experienced guide. They are essential in helping us realistically evaluate our life and the actions we have taken.

Once we have compiled this list, what are we supposed to do with it? We are to become "willing to make appropriate amends to them all." Who are we to make reparations to? The answer is "them all," not just some of them but everyone that we placed on our list. We are not allowed to eliminate individuals who we feel owe us amends. We are cleaning up our side of the street. What another individual does with their side of the street is absolutely none of our business. Also, please note that Step Eight specifies making appropriate amends, which is different from just saying "I'm sorry." Amends defines as "reparation or compensation." There is a big difference between an amends and an apology. The amends we make must be equivalent to the damage we caused, "appropriate".

The sequence of these Steps guides us on a path of Spiritual growth, concluding, hopefully, in a state of *God Realization*. Steps Eight and Nine come after Steps Four through Seven because getting ready to make amends, and then making amends for, our behavior will have no meaning if we continue to repeat the behavior we are making amends for. Steps Four through Seven give us the tools to help us not repeat our damaging behaviors.

When making your list it is strongly recommend that the first entry on that list is you, the list creator. Living any part of life under the influence of ego/self-will/shadow undeniably creates unparalleled damage in and to that life. Additionally, we cannot give away what we do not have. How can we truly make amends to others when we haven't genuinely given those amends to ourselves? Yes, we can go through the motions, but what are we seeking to achieve? Are we, as we learned in Step Five, looking to make a number three relationship into a number two, or worse, a number one? We do this when we allow another human being to influence of any aspect of ourselves.

STEP EIGHT WORKSHEET

1. *Write a brief statement,* in your own words, describing what the above explanation of Step Eight has taught you.

2. On a sheet of paper create four columns. Work Step Eight by going from listing an entity you have damaged in column one, to the damage you have caused that entity in column two, and the appropriate amends you feel guided to make to that entity in column three. This lets you seek the knowledge of your Higher Power's guidance for each entry with minimal difficulty, which allows you to better understand the damage that you are listing and the amends you intend to make. The utilization of the fourth column will be explained in the Step Nine worksheet section.

3. How will you know if you are willing to make amends?

STEP NINE

"We made direct appropriate amends to the individuals listed in Step Eight wherever possible, except when to do so would create more damage."

We have completed Step Eight, we have our list in hand, and we have become willing to make appropriate amends to everyone on our list. Do we simply attempt to contact everyone on our list and make the appropriate amends? As logical as that sounds the answer is "No!" The additional guidance we need before we embark on making our amends are given to us in the Ninth Step.

The first guidance the Ninth Step gives us is we are to make "direct appropriate amends". This means that if I owe amends to Al, I don't go to Bob and ask him to pass along my amends to Al. I go directly to Al. To whom are we going to make "direct appropriate amends"? To the "individuals listed in Step Eight." However, there are additional qualifying instructions we must apply before we take the action of making amends.

The first qualifying instruction is "wherever possible". This phrase can be defined as the ability or power to, without restrictions, accomplish a given task. These few words allow us not to hold ourselves to impossible standards. We do not diminish our overall efforts or the effectiveness of our amends, for example, if the person we need to make amends to is no longer alive, or if we have made an honest attempt to locate them and we cannot, or if we have made contact and they refuse to meet with us or hear what we have to say. We may also find ourselves in a situation where an individual may hear what we have to say and then reject and/or refuse to accept our amends. That is alright. Our job is to 'become willing" and to "make direct amends to the entities listed in Step Eight wherever possible." The "wherever possible" covers an individual's refusal to accept, or complete rejection of, our amends.

The next qualifying instruction is "except." "Except" tells us that there is another criteria to be met before we can make our amends. The qualifier is "when to do so would create more damage." The wisdom this phrase informs us of is that at the time we are to perform our amends we should not do or cause damage of any kind. Who are we being concerned with causing damage to by making our amends? The answer is anyone.

We are not working this Step of making amends to create further damage that would lead to a need for us to make future amends. Conversely, we are not to employ this final qualifier to relieve us of the responsibility of making amends to individuals on our list. There is no infallible way that will allow the individual working this Step to determine if making an amends will result in an injury. The best that we can do is to pray for guidance in this matter and have the faith to follow that guidance. Discussing any dilemmas that arise with an individual who has worked this Step is also highly recommended.

This Step can take an extended period of time to complete. In fact, due to our inability to connect with individuals on our list, we may never complete this Step as it was originally constructed. There will come a time when we need to redirect our efforts. With the guidance that we receive through prayer and the communications we have with someone who has worked this Step, we may come to a place where we realize that another course of action is needed. That course of action can be called "indirect amends." As an easy example, let's say we owe a financial amends to an individual. We cannot locate this individual. After a period of time, the length of which is arrived at through prayer and another experienced individual's input, we make a financial contribution to a local nonprofit in the exact amount of the amount owed the individual. There are infinite permutations that can arise in fulfilling this Step. That is why I emphasize prayer and communications with an experienced individual.

One last comment. God calls upon us to serve, not to sacrifice. Be aware of how much time and/or money you are committing to making amends at any one given time. Do not overextend yourself. Not living up to the amends we agree to, creates a dynamic that can intensify the strength of the voice of ego/self-will/shadow. We are best served by taking a bit longer to complete our amends then reneging on them.

STEP NINE WORKSHEET

1. *Write a brief statement,* in your own words, describing what the above explanation of Step Nine has taught you.

2. With your Step Eight worksheet in hand, you are now ready to make use of column four. This column will become your "direct/indirect" column. Based upon the guidance that you get in your prayers and conversations with a Step Nine-experienced individual, you will designate, for each entity listed, if you will be making direct or indirect amends. Ultimately, the Great Spirit is in charge so any determination you make regarding direct or indirect is always subject to revision. More is always revealed.

Just because you are working towards *God Realization* doesn't make you immune to the maneuverings of ego/self-will/shadow. Ego/self-will/shadow will always attempt to sabotage your efforts. Regarding this Step, one of the ways it will do this is to plant a suggestion in your mind that you can just, without pre-approval, basically ambush someone on your list and pour out your amends. "It's God's will for me, isn't it?" That is not the way this Step is intended to work. You need to first seek the entity's willingness to hear the amends. If your amends are with an individual you live with or see often, you can verbally ask the people their permission to make amends to them. You basically state, "I am working to improve myself, and in reviewing my life I have come to realize that I have, through action or inaction, caused damage to you. If you would be willing, at your convenience, I would like to make amends to you." If the answer is affirmative do not immediately start making your amends. Ask the person if you can set up a time and place that works for them. Attempt to accommodate their choice to the best of your ability, keeping in mind your schedule and allow for an additional period of conversation to be part of the process. Once the amends are made you can cross this individual off your Step Eight list. If they meet with you and refuse to accept your amends, you can still change their status on the Step Eight list. Remember that you have now fulfilled the Step Eight directive, "become willing to make amends," and also the "wherever possible" statement of this Step.

If someone you have become willing to make amends to is not a part of your everyday life and you know how to communicate with them indirectly, non-verbally (text messaging, email or regular mail), then do so with a version of the following statement: "I am working to improve myself and in reviewing my life I have come to realize that I have, through action or inaction, caused damage to you. If you would be willing, at your convenience, I would like to make amends to you. I am more than willing to set up a time and place that is convenient for you. I look forward to your response." As with the scenario in the previous paragraph, attempt to accommodate their choice to the best of your ability, keeping in mind your schedule and allowing for an additional period of conversation to be a part of the process. Once the amends are made you can cross this individual off your Step Eight list. If they meet with you and refuse to accept your amends, you can still change their status on the Step Eight list. Remember that you have fulfilled the Step Eight directive, "become willing to make amends," and also the "wherever possible" statement of this Step.

If an individual you have become willing to make amends to is not a part of your daily or everyday life, or you have no way of communicating with them, or should they deny your request to make direct amends to them, then in your Step Eight fourth column designate them as "indirect." If their status should change for any reason, you can adjust their designation accordingly. The indirect amends, whatever they are, can be made to society in general. You can make the appropriate, equivalent amends to your favorite charity or nonprofit. For instance, you can bundle a few of your indirect amends together and fulfill them by serving a meal at a local soup kitchen. As you complete your indirect amends you may remove the individual from your Step Eight list.

There may come a time where you sense that someone who has refused to accept your amends might benefit from a restatement of those amends, or there may come a time when someone you have made indirect amends to reappears in your life. In either case, there is no law that says your initial amends can't be restated. This is not about begging, so to speak, for someone's forgiveness or acceptance, it is about recognizing that someone is ready to move on in this aspect of their life, or that they have suddenly been placed in your path by The Creator for this very purpose.

Regarding the amends itself, remember this is about your behavior, not the other person's behavior. You may feel that they owe you an amends, but you are not here to work their program for them. You are here to work your own program. Clean your side of the street and leave their side of the street to them.

Lastly, keep your amends simple. State what you are making amends for and then state the amends as simply as possible. An example is: "There was nothing you ever did that warranted the way I treated you." The shorter, the simpler, the better.

STEP TEN

"We continued to set our Intentions to be in alignment with our Spiritual Beliefs and when our Awareness informs us of an inconsistency, we gently Intervene on ourselves."

IAI

Please note: The use of the terms "Spirit" and "God" in the following paragraphs are not meant to be misconstrued as over-riding your own belief system. The terms are being used generically. Feel free to substitute whatever name, term or phrase resonates with you.

The letters IAI stand for three parts of a process that allows us to change the way our brains react to stimuli. The letters stand for: Intention, Awareness and Intervention. It is strongly recommended that this process becomes incorporated into the practice you do the first thing every morning. These three components are specifically designed to achieve two objectives. The first objective is to start the practitioner off on their day centered in their Spirit instead of their Ego. This is based upon the belief that duality exists in each and every one of us. There is a Native American folk tale that best sums up my beliefs. In it a grandfather is lecturing his grandson, telling him that each human being is made up of two wolves, a good wolf and a bad wolf. The grandfather goes on to explain that the two wolves are in constant battle with each other. At this point the grandson asks, "Which wolf wins the battle?" The grandfather replies, "Whichever one you feed." I call the good wolf Spirit and the bad wolf ego/self-will/shadow. In the Twelve Step community, there is an acronym for Ego that is "Edging God Out." The second objective this practice achieves is to focus the brain, both the cognitive and non-cognitive sections, on new ways of responding instead of old ways of reacting.

Prayer is a very personal practice and differs from one person to another. There is no wrong way to pray. As Rumi once said, "There are a thousand ways to kneel and kiss the ground." What I believe this means is that each and every one of us are one with the Creator. Therefore, everything we think, feel, say and do are transmitted instantaneously to the Creator. What distinguishes prayer from other forms of communications is having the intention of wanting the Creator to be addressed. There is one thing I have learned about praying that I would like to pass on to you. It is that all prayers should be an expression of gratitude and not a request. We should start each of our prayers with a phrase such as "Thank you God for" instead of "God, please give me." The expression of gratitude accomplishes two things. First, it doesn't presume that we know better than God what we need. The second is that it implies a state of abundance as opposed to a condition of lacking. The following are the intentional prayers I recommend saying on a daily basis. I recommend always starting with a prayer that affirms our Divinity. The reason for starting this way is that it immediately lifts us out of our default lower state of existence, ego/self-will/shadow, and into our optional higher state of existence, Spirit. The prayers in the following intentions are being listed as suggestions only. You are a Child of the Creator, create your own or feel free to use mine or some combination thereof.

IAI - The Practice

Intention:

Our actions create the reality of our lives. There are two powerful tools that we possess that guide our actions: our beliefs and our intentions. There are several ways we can state our intentions. There is prayer, affirmation, contemplation, and just plain conversation. The key to any form of transmission is that it is intended as a message from ourselves to our Higher Power. I recommend always starting with a statement that affirms our Divinity. The reason for starting this way is that we are immediately lifted out of our default lower state of existence, ego/self-will/shadow, and into our optional higher state of existence, Spirit. After that I suggest starting with a couple of intentions that are demonstrations of the Divinity that we are acknowledging.

To start with I suggest setting the following four intentions.

1st: Acknowledge your own Divinity, in any way you are comfortable doing so. (Example; I am One with God in Love and Light.)

2nd: Is a demonstration of your Divinity by intending to practice, as best as you can, unconditional love for yourself and others. (Example; Thank you God for showing me how to be unconditionally loving of myself and others.)

3rd: Is a demonstration of your unconditional love (2nd intention) by intending to practice, as best as possible, forgiveness for yourself and others. (example: Thank you God for showing me how to be forgiving of myself and others.)

4th: Intend to eliminate a behavior that is interfering with your ability to live a serene and joyous life. (example: Thank you God for removing the obsession and compulsion to act out in anger today.)

This is the minimal practice. Additional spiritual practice after these four intentional prayers is definitely encouraged. Treat your Spirit as a muscle. The more you exercise it the stronger it becomes.

Awareness:

This means, as best as you can throughout your waking hours, being as aware as possible, of your thoughts, feelings and actions. Anytime your awareness shows you that you are going against any of your morning intentions, you go to the third letter, the second "I." The IAI's awareness component brings an additional blessing. As we raise our awareness during the day, we are training ourselves to be more aware during our meditation. When we become more aware in meditation it facilitates our spending more time in quiet then chatter. As we become more aware of chatter in our meditation, we are training ourselves to be more self-aware during the day, showing us more quickly when we are not living up to our intentions. The cross pollination will continue to work as long as we are practicing both components.

Intervention:

When you become aware that you are going against your intentions, you need to intervene on yourself. You need to do this gently. If you are not gentle with yourself, not only are you going against your intentions, you are creating an atmosphere that will perpetuate the behavior you want to intervene on. An example of a gentle intervention is, "Stop, this doesn't serve me anymore." After you state your intervention you then repeat the morning intention that you are not complying with until your thought, feeling and/or action is back in compliance with your morning intention. You may find yourself intervening numerous times throughout your day. This is alright. This indicates that you are becoming more aware. The need for intervention has always been there, it's just you were so accepting of the ego chatter you didn't see that it wasn't serving you. The above description of the IAI is just the starting point, not the entire path. Spiritual practice is not meant to be complex or complicated. Spiritual practice is meant to be simple though it may not always be easy. The simplification of the IAI comes in the Intention and Intervention sections. We can combine the four intentions stated above into one intention, such as this paraphrase of an Emanuel Swedenborg teaching: "My job is to act as if God was supposed to show up but couldn't make it and asked me to take its place." Or as Edgar Cayce said (reading 5392-1, paragraph 8, given August 28, 1944) "Use the power thus generated – not to self-indulgence – but to beautify, but make the world a better place because ye have lived in it."

STEP TEN WORKSHEET

Write a brief statement, in your own words, describing what the above explanation of Step Ten has taught you.

STEP ELEVEN

"We sought through meditation and prayer to advance our conscious communication with God as we understood God, pursuing only the knowledge of God's will for us and the willingness to carry that out."

The 12 Steps, being Divinely designed, teach at multiple levels and provide a deeper connected lesson at each level. Besides the individual lessons encompassed by each step, in their entirety the 12 Steps provide two different but associated journey lessons. The first journey lesson is the transformation from a self-centered vision of life, as identified in Step One, to a vision of selfless service, taught in Step Twelve. The second journey lesson, parallels at a higher plane the first journey. It guides us from following a false Deity, ego/self-will/shadow, as identified in Step One to being guided by the only real and true Deity as identified in Step Twelve.

The Steps facilitate the above described dual journey lessons through a systematic approach of giving us the gift of meeting ourselves in the various aspects/obstacles impeding our *God Realization*. Step One introduces us to the major impediment to our *God Realization*, ego/self-will/shadow and how ego/self-will/shadow's voice has provided us with harsh lessons when we allowed it to guide us. Next up, Steps Two and Three are a set. Step Two introduces us to the voice that teaches the gentle lessons, which provides us with an unconditionally loving alternative to the harsh lesson of the Step One voice. Step Three instructs us to start recognizing that unconditionally loving voice and allowing that voice, that provides us with gentle lessons, to guide our actions and starts us on the path of *God Realization*. Steps Four through Seven are another set. They guide us in creating a new collection of spiritually based responses to the life on life terms we experience on our *God Realization* journey. In Step Four we meet ourselves from the perspective of defining what the Step Three phrase "turning our will and our life over to the care of a Power greater than ourselves" means. Step Five provides us with both the commitment to live our inventory as we outlined it in Step Four and the prioritization sequence of our relationships. Steps Six and Seven teach us how to deal with ego/self-will/shadow's attempt to intercede on our carrying out our Step Five commitment. The next Step set we encounter are Steps Eight and Nine. These two Steps guide us in identifying and clearing up the damage we inflicted on others during our acting out under the influence of ego/self-will/shadow. Step Ten stands on its own. It transits us from a state of Spiritual Awareness to a state of Spiritual Awakeness. It accomplishes this by providing us with a gentle yet effective tool to return us to the path of *God Realization* when our mindfulness reveals to us that we have found our way back to allowing ego/self-will/shadow to influence us on our journey. Step Ten is the gateway to the Spiritual Awakeness the Steps are designed to guide us through.

Step Eleven facilitates our Spiritual evolutionary journey from Awakeness to *God Realization*. It is very explicit in its directive as to how to accomplish this transformation. Starting with the word "We" as all the previous Steps do, reminds us that this is not a trek done solo. Every one of us are Spiritual Beings encased in a human body walking this path with individuals of like mind and like kind. There is a Taoist teaching that states "There is only one path and we all walk it". It goes on to further state "there are only two types of people on the path, those who are ahead of us and those who are behind us". The tale concludes by directing us that "when we encounter an individual who is ahead of us on the path we are instructed to be humble and ask them to teach us and when we encounter an individual behind us on the path we are to be compassionate and offer to instruct them."

Unlike the previous ten Steps that are backward-looking Steps, Steps that have us review our lives, behaviors and interactions, Step Eleven brings us directly into the present moment, the now. It achieves this by directing us to the in the now practices of, "meditation and prayer". Even though the Twelve Steps are a guide to *God Realization* this is the first time a Step directs us to the Spirit enhancing practices of "meditation and prayer". Up until Step Eleven the practices of "meditation and prayer" are tools that are utilized as a way to resolve issues uncovered through our working of the Steps. Now we are being guided to utilize "meditation and prayer" to be preventative instead of curative. What are the spiritual practices of "meditation and prayer" guiding us to achieve? Meditation is the tool of spiritual self-examination, the meeting and familiarizing us with the Divine Presence within us. Prayer is the tool that communicates our expression of gratitude for that Divine Presence in our lives. What is the combination of these two powerful Spiritual tools in a single Step guiding us to achieve? The answer is "to advance our conscious communication with God as we understood God."

What do we need to do in order to achieve this advancement? What is the goal of this advancement? The answers to these two questions are given to us as the next guidance in the wording of the Step, "pursuing only the knowledge of God's will for us." If, as we came to believe in Step Two, that "a Power greater than ourselves" is all-powerful, all-knowing, ever present and unconditionally loving why wouldn't we seek out this entity's guidance?

Before we complete this Step, there is one more factor that we are being instructed to pursue: "the power to carry that out." With this statement we are being informed that familiarity with the facts regarding God's will for us is not sufficient. Whereas Step Three puts into action the beliefs we come to in Step Two, Step Eleven combines the beliefs and the corresponding action in its final phrase. There is, I believe, a three-tier Divine Law, which informs us that knowledge without action produces nothing. Knowledge coupled with unspiritual action that results from listening to the voice of ego/self-will/shadow, will ultimately produce disharmony and chaos. Knowledge coupled with the Spirit-guided appropriate action facilitates the transformation from Spiritual Awareness to Spiritual Awakeness to *God Realization*.

The Power we seek comes from within us, growing stronger as we exercise our free will to choose to listen to and act on the direction given by the internal Voice of Spirit, the Giver of the gentle lesson. The more we come to rely on the guidance that Divine Wisdom provides for us, the more we experience the serenity that comes with being in Harmony with God's Will for us. Ultimately the Power we seek is the Power we build. This Power reflects the cumulative acceptance, faith and trust we have developed in the Spiritually enhancing rightness of the outcomes we experienced when we were aligned with God's Will for us.

The depth of the teachings, the gifts that Step Eleven provides us with don't stop with the above explanation of an aspect of the Law of Cause and Effect. Step Eleven teaches us how to grow as Spiritual beings. It does this by emphasizing the tools of meditation and prayer. One of the benefits that meditation facilitates is the enhanced awareness that our ego/self-will/shadow is actively attempting to hijack our connection with Spirit. This awareness enhances our ability to recognize ego/self-will/shadow's activity in our day-to-day lives. Conversely, the ability to recognize the activity of ego/self-will/shadow in our daily lives enhances our ability to recognize ego/self-will/shadow's activity in our meditation.

What do we do when we find ourselves actively engaging with ego/self-will/shadow? We return our focus to The Divine. This is done through prayer. Prayer is an umbrella term that encompasses all forms of communication with The Divine. Being one with The Creator, anything we do is a communication with The Creator. Any communication with The Creator is therefore a prayer. Our actions, our thoughts, and our emotions are all instantaneously transmitted to The Creator and therefore meet the definition of prayer. In meditation, we are taught to re-center by implementing any one of a number of methods. The re-centering can take the form of a visualization, a mantra or following our breath, just to name a few. Like meditation, prayer is enhanced the more we use re-centering in our meditation. This enhances our ability to use prayer throughout our day-to-day activities. Re-centering during our daily living enhances our ability to use it in our meditation.

The tools of meditation and prayer are the basis of recognizing and transforming when we are in need of implementing our Step Six and/or Step Seven. The interconnectivity and cross pollination between the Steps, that is built into the Steps, is truly Divine.

STEP ELEVEN WORKSHEET

1. *Write a brief statement,* in your own words, describing what the above explanation of Step Eleven has taught you.

2. Ego/self-will/shadow is our default state of being. We are designed to desire to bring to the forefront the Divine Essence we possess, hence Step Eleven. It is suggested that the best way you can start your day is with Spiritual practice. Why start your day with ego/self-will/shadow as your guiding voice?

3. Create a first thing-upon-awakening Spiritual practice that incorporates meditation, prayer and maybe some Spiritual reading and contemplation (deep reflective thought). This practice will connect you with the Deity within you, which will facilitate your awareness of the knowledge of God's will for you and connect you with the power to carry it out. The Sufi mystic Rumi once said (as per brainyquote.com): "There are a thousand ways to kneel and kiss the ground; there are a thousand ways to go home again." Keep in mind, it's not your form that matters. Your form, your practice will continue to change, to evolve. It will always be your beliefs and intentions that create your reality.

4. Create a prayer that you can utilize during the times you may not be able to, for whatever reason, enact your first thing-in-the-morning practices and/or are unsure of God's will for you. Simplicity is Spiritual. May I suggest "God thank you for showing me where my greatest good will be made manifest." God is always the first responder, however, God does not have to explain itself so God's responses will always be, as stated in the King James Bible (3 Kings, chapter 19, verse 12), "And after the earthquake a fire; but the LORD was not in the fire: and after the fire a still small voice."

As soon as the still, small voice of the Divine Response has completed, then the voice of ego/self-will/shadow will start up. It will attempt to confuse you so that you will no longer retain the guidance that The Divine has given you. It will utilize whatever diversionary tactics it can. This is where all the work you have done on the prior

Steps comes into play. Your ability to distinguish the energy/flavor/taste sensation of Spirit as opposed to the energy/flavor/taste sensation of ego/self-will/shadow is the key. Hold onto the knowledge that the still, small voice imparts to you and with the faith and trust you have developed over the course of your working your Steps, take the appropriate action or inaction. If for whatever reason after your first attempt to ascertain God's will for you, you are unsure of it you can repeat this prayer process.

If a repeated attempt doesn't provide you with a satisfactory level of clarity you can utilize a stream of consciousness technique. At the top of a piece of paper or Word document write the question that you are seeking to have answered. Say a prayer of guidance before you start writing. Then just write. Don't attempt to answer the question. Just write, anything. Eventually your Divine consciousness will kick in and the answer to your question will flow through to the document you have created.

STEP TWELVE

"We, experiencing *God Realization* as the product of applying these steps in our lives, continually carry this message to our fellow spiritual beings and demonstrate our God-Realized Nature in all our affairs."

How do we verify that we are growing on our path to *God Realization*? With this Step. We are acknowledging and becoming fully aware of the fact that we are Divine in our core nature. In a deep sense, Step 12 is both the completion of a spiritual journey and the beginning of a more advanced Spiritual journey. The journey completed is the one through the 12 Steps. It guided us in raising and enhancing our awareness of our Divine origin and nature. We revisit any of the first 11 Steps only when we are experiencing our will being hijacked by the voice of harsh lessons, the voice of ego/self-will/shadow. Step 12 is designed to be a Step without an end. This is the advanced Spiritual journey, an ongoing demonstration of our *God Realization*.

The Twelfth Step informs us how we came to experience and will continue to enhance our *"God Realization"*: as the product of applying these steps in our lives. What we are applying are the lessons the previous Eleven Steps have imprinted on our Spirit. What are the results of "applying these steps in our lives?" Again, the Divine wisdom incorporated into these Twelve Steps has the answer, giving us a dual directive. The first directive is our instruction regarding our relationship to the collective, to "continually carry this message to our fellow spiritual beings," while the second part is instruction for self-application: "demonstrate our God-Realized Nature in all our affairs."

The first directive, "continually carry this message to our fellow Spiritual beings," teaches us to do so "continually," without interruption! What are we carrying to our fellow Spiritual beings? The message is the path we traveled to experience *God Realization*, these Twelve Steps. This first directive guides us out of ourselves. It reinforces the Spiritual concept that we are here to serve, that we keep what we have, then enhance what we have, by selflessly giving it away.

Because we can't give away what we don't have, the second directive is about ourselves, that we must "demonstrate our God-Realized Nature in all our affairs." What we are demonstrating is the existence of "our God-Realized Nature." The final instruction, the last unanswered question that the Twelve Steps resolves for us is, "When do we demonstrate the existence of our *God Realization* nature?" The answer is simple "in all our affairs." We are not to make our demonstration based upon a particular situation, when it will benefit us or creates the illusion that we are something we are not. We are to make our demonstration in whatever situation or subject we are dealing with. We are being directed to walk our talk. The state of *God Realization* cannot be sustained and nurtured if we are being guided by ego/self-will/shadow.

As the final step, Step Twelve creates the tone for the preceding eleven steps by establishing their collective destination. For our newly created fellowship the goal is precise; *God Realization*. It also tells us that the path to *God Realization* is equally precise; the result of applying the preceding eleven steps in our lives. Step Twelve also informs us that we are all equal. We are all spiritual beings and the only qualification for *God Realization* is the implementation of the lessons the Twelve Steps provide in our lives. This means that the God presence is already within is, waiting to be realized. It also teaches that our gender, race, religion, nationality, age, lifestyle, material possessions and any other ego/self-will/shadow-based qualifiers are irrelevant. We are Divine and this cannot be taken from us, it just patiently awaits our realization of it.

Another teaching of this step is that our goal has nothing to do with the ego/self-will/shadow aspects of our being. We are not doing this work with the Twelve Steps to become intellectually superior, emotionally stable nor behaviorally modified. We are solely seeking *God Realization*. There is nothing more and we are not aiming for anything less. The paradox of this step is that, as we grow in our *God Realization*, we will obtain intellectual depth, emotional stability and become behaviorally modified. This happens because as we proceed on this path of *God Realization*, we transcend the physical/material realm and are governed by a higher set of laws, God's Laws, as they are made manifest and applied in the spiritual realm. The individual *God Realization* we develop unifies us on a higher plane of consciousness, the Spiritual Realm. Depending upon where we are in our development, we override more and more of our base human nature, in a sense creating Heaven on Earth.

These Twelve Steps are guideposts on a journey. Even the final guidepost, the Twelfth Step—what to do with our achieving *God Realization*—isn't a destination, it is the beginning of another, more remarkable journey. Remember, our Higher Power is "a power capable of accomplishing things that are beyond our ability to imagine and/or comprehend."

STEP TWELVE WORKSHEET

Write a brief statement, in your own words, describing what the above explanation of Step Twelve has taught you. Please pay special attention to the term *"God Realization."*

The process that facilitated your journey to *God Realization* doesn't cease to be relevant because you have completed working the Twelve Steps. Just the opposite. Remember, you are on a journey that has no end. To continue to grow in your *God Realization* you must continue to do the work that brought you there. Practice, practice, practice.

The Twelve Traditions: Reworded and Explained

The Twelve Steps guide us, with our permission and participation, to an awareness of how ego/self-will/shadow works in our personal lives and then provide us with the tools necessary to overcome it. So, you must work the Twelve Traditions. The Traditions differ from the Steps in that they guide us to an awareness of how the ego/self-will/shadow is working in the arena of our collective consciousness, as well as provide us with the guidance to recognize and overcome it.

TRADITION ONE

*"The common good must, always, come first; God Realization
depends upon the harmony within the collective."*

With each of the Twelve Steps, we are reminded that this journey towards *God Realization* is not a path walked solo. And just as the Twelve Steps are guideposts on this excursion so are the Twelve Traditions. This amalgamation of guideposts known as the Twelve Traditions reveals to us the manifestations of ego/self-will/shadow uniquely applicable to the collective. Along with those revelations comes the Spiritual antidote for each and every one of them. With the guidance provided and the application performed we can build a community, the collective, which will perfectly support us in the *God Realization* work we are engaged in.

This First Tradition reinforces the importance of the collective; "The common good must, always, come first." This is a powerful, definitive statement. The importance, the prerequisite of the common good is, in a sense, the prime directive. The collective must sustain its harmony for the individual members to grow in Spirit. This doesn't mean that the members of the collective cannot disagree with one another. However, what they mustn't do is allow the disagreement to become divisive to the collective.

How does the collective achieve and sustain the harmony that is so essential to the personal *God Realization* process? The Second Tradition provides us with the answer to that question.

TRADITION TWO

"For the collective's purpose, there is but one ultimate authority — an unconditionally loving God as The Divine may reveal
Itself in the collective's conscience. The collective's leaders are
but trusted servants; they do not govern."

Because of Divine guidance, the collective's harmony will only
come into being by having a united sense of purpose and a unified vision
of the path to follow. If it were left up to the guidance provided by each
member's best thinking as filtered through their ego/self-will/shadow,
the collective's best thinking would result in chaos. How can unity be
achieved when the voices of ego/self-will/shadow, only concerned with
self, are the only voices being listened to? The Second Tradition provides
the collective with the Spiritual counterpoint to the dysfunction provided
by ego/self-will/shadow, so that the collective communally seeks The
Divine's unconditionally loving guidance about any issue.

Since there is ultimately only one consciousness, the collective can
only arrive at one undivided conclusion. If the collective cannot reach a
unanimous consensus, then it should take no action. Every member of
the collective should then return to their consciousness-seeking practice
and reconsider the subject. This process is not about a majority rules
decision. The majority rules decision-making process reflects the ego/
self-will/shadow, not the Oneness of the Divine. The collective may find
that the minority, or even a singularly held opinion, is, in due course,
the source of the collective's direction on an issue.

The Second Tradition goes a huge step further to ensure collective
harmony. It instructs that the collective's leaders are trusted servants,
not governors. It creates an inverted power authority pyramid. The
titular head of the collective as defined by this construct is the leading
servant. This individual has the authority to act only when instructed by
the collective, utilizing only the power the collective has granted them.

At the beginning of the collective's journey, the need for a leader is
minimal. As the collective advances on its path, the need for leadership
wanes and then vanishes.

TRADITION THREE

"The only requirement for becoming a member of the collective is the desire to work towards *God Realization* within the collective."

Just as the Twelfth Step eliminates any non-spiritual qualifier for achieving *God Realization*, so does the Third Tradition eliminate any non-spiritual qualifier for becoming a member of a *God Realization* seeking collective.

The Third Tradition takes the above qualifier a step further. Any individual seeking membership in the collective need only have the desire to work towards *God Realization*, they don't have to actively be engaged in the work. And that individual seeking membership is the sole determiner of their desire. In other words, no human being nor group of human beings, no matter how advanced they are on the *God Realization* path, can ascertain another individual's calling. That is, always, between the individual and their God.

To extend this qualifier further, only the individual having stated the qualifying desire for membership can revoke their membership. Membership, like desire, is not subject to the determination of any other individual or group of individuals. This too is between the individual and their God.

TRADITION FOUR

"Every collective must always remain autonomous."

The Fourth Tradition is short on words but is an enormously significant tradition. There must be no doubt about what this Tradition is teaching. Each collective should never, regardless of the circumstances, have any connection to, or engagement in any form of collaboration with, any other collective. Each collective must always start, stand, grow and fold entirely on its own. To do otherwise—to connect and/or collaborate with another collective—would start both collectives down a path that would change its focus from being a Spiritual society working towards *God Realization* to a religious congregation that creates dogma and ritual to distinguish itself from other collectives. For a prime example of this dynamic, you can research the destructive relationship between early Roman Catholicism and the various Gnostic practices.

TRADITION FIVE

"Each collective has only one purpose and one purpose only — to aid in and support the process of *God Realization* for all its members, uniformly."

The Fifth Tradition sets the parameters for the collective's sole focus, to assist each member of the collective in their quest for *God Realization*. Any other purpose is a distraction and a diversion from focusing on that which has eternal implications to that which is impermanent, affecting at most this lifetime. The more the collective focuses its energies on *God Realization* the less significant distractions of the physical realm will appear.

The Fifth Tradition teaches another important directive; that the collective serves all its members equally. As taught in the Twelfth Step, every human being is, at the essence, an equal Child of the Divine. This understanding of equality compels us to travel the road to *God Realization* side by side with our collective family. If one family member of the collective has trouble with a teaching or a practice, it is imperative that the collective work with that family member until they are at pace with the rest of the collective. There can be no greater demonstration of *God Realization* than entering into and acknowledging The Oneness of all The Creator's creations.

TRADITION SIX

"The collective should never, ever, support in anyway any other collective or external venture. Doing so will produce entanglements in the physical realm created by the attachment to nonpermanent materialistic objects which will divert the collective from its singular, *God Realization*, purpose."

The Sixth Tradition is an expansive clarification of the Fourth and Fifth Traditions. It tells how to identify what would violate the autonomous directive to the collective of the Fourth Tradition, as well as that which falls outside the collective's singular sole purpose Fifth Tradition directive—the obtainment of *God Realization*.

Ego/self-will/shadow starts by planting a seed of non-*God Realization* distraction within an individual collective member and attempts to spread this diversion to the collective. It will cause the collective to misconstrue something that has no bearing on the process of *God Realization* as being worthy of entanglement or engagement.

Beware. The previous and subsequent guidelines are not negotiable. At the moment, these guidelines become negotiable they have been hijacked by a singular or combined ego/self-will/shadow.

TRADITION SEVEN

"Every collective ought to be totally self-supporting, declining contributions from non-collective members. Self-supporting should be equally distributed between the collective members with no member willingly or unwillingly shouldering a disproportionate burden."

The consistent thread that runs through these Traditions is continuous identifying and defining of various applications of the Fourth Tradition directive of being "autonomous." In the Seventh Tradition, we are directed not to accept any form of contribution that is not from a collective member. Any contribution from a non-collective member can generate an indebtedness that will, eventually, create more problems than it will solve.

When we consider the structure of the collective and its needs, this tradition shouldn't impose any undue restrictions on the collective. Since the collective is aiming for *God Realization*, the acquisition of materialistic possessions is counter-productive to the collective's ultimate purpose. Once material possessions have been eliminated as an attainment goal, what contributions will the collective need? Literature to study? This might be desirable but isn't crucial. Beverages and snacks for the collective's meetings? A nice touch but not essential. Rent for the meeting place? Not necessary, since renting a place will eventually lead to wanting to own a facility. This will create the dysfunctional dynamic that has contributed to making our modern religions the out-of-focus practices they have become. The collective, in the spirit of not creating a disproportionate burden, should rotate its meetings between its member's abodes.

Ultimately, the Seventh Tradition defines simplicity for the collective by guiding the it to narrow its focus on its sole purpose, *God Realization*.

TRADITION EIGHT

"Each collective should remain forever non-professional."

The Eighth Tradition informs the collective as to the positional, functional make-up of the collective. There are to be no professionals empowered to make decisions for the collective. Individual collective members may have an expertise that supports them in the material world. That expertise may be shared with the collective but never implemented without the acceptance of the collective, as outlined in the Second Tradition.

TRADITION NINE

"Each collective should never be organized."

This tradition, like the one that proceeds it, states the obvious. What needs to be organized? If the Divine is everything, then what is One needs no organization. The obvious only becomes obvious with experience. In order to guide the collective in its early stages of development these Traditions have been created. As the collective matures the guidance provided by the Second Tradition becomes the source of all decision-making. The other traditions aren't overwritten; they are always applicable and valid. As the collective grows, the necessary decisions will be directly related to obtaining *God Realization*, not topics covered in the Ninth Tradition.

TRADITION TEN

"The collective will have no opinion and will take no stance on material world, non-collective related issues; consequently, the collective will never be drawn into dispute or distraction."

There is no more important effort that the collective can make than to engage in *God Realization* work. Having an opinion, taking a stance on worldly issues, will not only distract the collective from its Fifth Tradition mandate, it will set the wrong example for the material world. By demonstrating the non-attachment to worldly issues that comes with the pursuit of *God Realization*, the collective bestows its greatest good on society.

Individual members of the collective may have opinions on material world, non-collective related issues. The individual's karma may be such that they are guided to engage in those types of issues. However, the individual must never profess to represent or speak for the collective.

TRADITION ELEVEN

"The collective should never have a public relations person nor policy. The collective membership will grow in numbers due to individuals being attracted to the collective rather than the collective being promoted to the individual. Members of the collective should never acknowledge their collective membership at the public level."

The definition of promotion, per Google, is an "activity that supports or provides active encouragement for the furtherance of a cause, venture, or aim." To promote a collective in any way, shape or form will hijack the collective into becoming another, newer version of the religious establishments the collective has been formed to transcend.

Divine Presence will send the collective the members it is supposed to have at the time they are supposed to be there. They will be presented to an existing collective member as a seeker of the source behind that member's social demonstration.

As the collective grows spiritually, as each member advances closer to *God Realization*, the concept of being entangled in the material world behind the effort of promotion is increasingly recognized as an act of insanity, a contradiction of concepts. Trust God to achieve exactly the right results at exactly the right time. *God Realization* is not about getting in God's way, it's about getting out of God's way so that the individual can become at One with the Creator.

TRADITION TWELVE

"Egolessness is the transcendent underpinning of all of these Twelve Traditions, continuously reminding the members of the collective to place Divinely inspired ethics, morals and actions before ego/self-will/shadow originating guidance."

This Tradition is easier said than done, especially in the early stages of the *God Realization* process. There is no such thing as failure, so don't allow yourself to be guided to fear failure or to avoid it. Our life is our textbook; it provides our lessons. We are both the teacher and the student. As the teacher, we choose the lessons we experience and as the student we choose whether we will do the work the lesson requires of us in order to master the lesson. Sometimes our lessons overlap, sometimes they are sequential. Sometimes our lessons are singular in nature, sometimes they are multi-level in nature. We are only teaching ourselves what we have come to this classroom to learn. Each lesson is designed to further our soul development, following the spiritual path we have chosen to expedite our reunification with The Creator. Because we are at one with the all-knowing, we can never, ever, give ourselves a lesson that we didn't need or we weren't fully equipped to take. We do, however, get to choose how many times we revisit the same lesson. The determining factor is: What voice are we listening to? If the Twelfth Tradition sounds a lot like the Third Step that's because it is. The Twelfth Tradition is the Third Step for the collective.

Whether singularly or collectively, the most important action in our spiritual growth is "What voice are we listening to and acting behind"? The individual enhances the collective and the collective enhances the individual. Learn to trust that still, small voice. You'll never regret it.

THE GOD TRILOGY

Book 1 is titled *"GOD IS"*; subtitled *"And I thought It Was All About Me, The Gospel of Rev. Phil"*. *"GOD IS"* is my Spiritual Autobiography. Its purpose is to provide you with the basis of believing that there is a Power greater than yourself that is not only watching over you but is willing and capable of intervening in your life for your betterment. This is a spiritual story not a religious one. The journey I will share with you is my own. It starts with an abusive, dysfunctional childhood which leads to a chaotic, anger filled, toxic adulthood. Due to interventions by a Deity I didn't even believe in, I not only survived my self-destructiveness I was able to turn my life around. This process connected me with a few unbelievable teachers and many cherished guides. What I learned along the path I document in this autobiography. I'll share with you my lessons and understandings, my Gospel, and cover the subjects of karma, God's grace, charity, mercy, true spirituality and above all, unconditional love. My hope is that this volume will stimulate you to seek out the source and inspiration of my transformation in your own life.

Book 2 is titled *"GOD REALIZATION."* *"GOD REALIZATION"* looks at the current state of religion and why I believe it is a broken concept. The impact of marketing a non-quantifiable product is explored. *"GOD REALIZATION"* will provide the reader with a Vedic concept known as Yuga, The Cycle of Ages and how that dynamic impacts the various religious traditions. *"GOD REALIZATION"* will look at why I believe the Eastern religions are so different from the Western religions. It will assess the influence of the foundational hunter-gatherer culture on the Abrahamic traditions. *"GOD REALIZATION"* will also, above all else, provide an alternative to the perceived problem. *"GOD REALIZATION"* is mainly a how-to guide that directs you in the process of reaching and connecting with the Divine Presence in your being, which is the proposed solution to the problems presented in the first part of the book. This guide is based on the 12 Step model but is structured to lead you to a deeper level spiritual connection than the traditional, behavior modification oriented, 12 Step programs. This book includes worksheets for each of the Steps and an interpretation of the 12 Traditions that will allow you, the reader, to form your own supportive spiritual fellowship.

Book 3 is titled *"GOD HEALS"*. Having been introduced to and then embracing the Divine Presence within yourself, as revealed in book 1, *"GOD IS,"* and then by following the guidance provided in book 2, *"GOD REALIZATION,"* you have made Spirit the guiding force in your life. We are then led to ask the question, "what do I do with this realization"? *"GOD HEALS"* provides one important answer to that question. It will look at how a deep belief in The Creator has been used not only to control one's body but to heal individuals with life threatening physical and mental disorders. This volume will review healing practices throughout the course of time and provide firsthand accounts of individuals applying spiritual beliefs and practices to facilitate their own ailments.

LOVE & LIGHT,
Rev. Phil

THE COMPANION TO
THE GOD TRILOGY

God Speaks is the fourth book in this series, and is a Companion to the God Trilogy. Buddha, in the Dhammapada (The Path of Eternal Truth), as translated by J. Richards, Chapter 6, "The Wise", Paragraph 5, is quoted as saying "As a deep lake is clear and calm, so the wise become tranquil after they listened to the truth." In the New Testament, the King James Bible version, The Gospel According to Saint Mark, Chapter 4, Verse 9, Jesus is quoted as saying "He that hath ears to hear, let him hear." Buddha and Jesus both asked their disciples to heed their teachings, to grow in Spirit. Spirit is like any muscle in the body. If you use it, it grows stronger. If you don't use it, it atrophies. *"GOD SPEAKS"*, was written with the sole purpose of being a spiritual muscle builder. This book contains a spiritual teaching for each day of the year. To further aide you, each teaching will have a contemplative commentary accompanying it. In "The Bhagavad Gita" (The Song of the Lord), as translated by Edwin Arnold, Chapter 18, "Of Religion by Deliverance and Renunciation", Paragraph 19, Lord Krishna imparts to Arjuna "Listen! tell thee for thy comfort this."

Enjoy more from Rev. Phil!

God IS: And I thought it was all about me
The God Trilogy – Book 1

I write this book, *GOD IS*, not as a speculator or as a spectator; I write about my experiences. I present this book as a gift to you, just as the spiritual experiences I share with you were gifted to me.

God Heals: The Power to Heal is Within
The God Trilogy – Book 3

GOD HEALS will look at how a deep belief in The Creator has been used not only to control one's body but to heal individuals with life threatening physical and mental disorders.

God Speaks: "In the beginning there was the word..." Om
The God Trilogy Companion –
Daily Contemplations

Buddha, in the Dhammapada (The Path of Eternal Truth), is quoted as saying "As a deep lake is clear and calm, so the wise become tranquil after they listened to the truth."

Church of the One God
www.ChurchOfTheOneGod.org